Lifelines FIVE

JOHN FOSTER

with PETER STEWART

COLLINS
EDUCATIONAL

INTRODUCTION

Lifelines is a series of five books providing a course in social and personal development for all 11-17-year olds. The books can be used on a year-by-year basis, but the structure is sufficiently flexible to allow teachers to use the sections selectively. The books can, therefore, easily be used with a school's own social education course in whatever way individual teachers think best.

Each book deals with a number of carefully selected topics, each divided into a series of double-page units. Each unit provides enough material for a weekly social education session. The activities are carefully structured so that individual work, pair work and group work can easily lead into or be developed out of whole class discussions. The approach is active – learning by doing and discussing — and the activities are designed so that they can take place in an ordinary classroom.

Each unit contains specific suggestions for individual follow-up activities, so that a folder of work can be built up. A number of the units provide individuals with the opportunity to reflect on their progress and thus to take more responsiblity for their own learning. These units act as an on-going form of personal recording and self-assessment. They can be used in conjunction with whatever scheme for recording personal progress and achievement a school is developing.

John L. Foster, Oxford 1988

Collins Educational, 8 Grafton Street, London W1X 3LA

© John Foster 1988
First published 1988

ISBN 0 00 327439 X

Designed by Glynis Edwards

Typeset by Chambers Wallace Ltd, London

Printed and bound by
Butler & Tanner Ltd, Frome, Somerset

CONTENTS

What is love?

LOVE OR OBSESSION?

'FOR THE FIRST MONTH AFTER I MET WENDY, I was convinced I was in love. I was completely obsessed with her. She was much prettier than any other girlfriend I'd had and when my friends saw me with her, they were green with envy. Then, after the initial excitement, I started noticing things about her I didn't really like: for instance, the way she'd be offhand when it was just the two of us and all over me when her friends were about. And the way she'd ramble on and on about what she'd been up to during the day, and then look bored when I told her what I'd been doing.

Looking back, I know that I didn't really love Wendy. I loved the way she looked, I loved the way my friends reacted when they saw us together, and I loved the idea of being in love. But it didn't go much further than that. It took me months before I really grew to love my present girlfriend, and I didn't even fancy her when we first met.

I think that when you really like someone as a person, their appearance doesn't even enter in to it. An ordinary looking girl, who you totally trust and feel completely comfortable with, can seem really beautiful in your eyes. And a gorgeous girl with an ugly personality becomes grotesque when you find out what she's like underneath.'

Paul, aged 20.

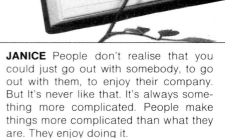

LIKING
OR
LOVING

JANICE Love? Well, I don't know what the word means. To me, I'm not sure that it really means anything. Well, it hasn't so far in my life. Not love for a person of my age or a similar age. Love for my parents, yes, but . . .

TINA What about that boy you were going out with? You said you were in love with him.

JANICE Oh yes, that was because he'd brainwashed me into thinking I was in love with him. Whereas all the time I wasn't. But now I've got everything straight about that. I know that kind of thing won't ever happen again. But when love does come along, I shall know.

TINA Yes, it's usually if the boy keeps saying he loves you, you tend to say it back sometimes, but you don't mean it. And then you get to a pitch where you daren't not say it, but all the time you don't mean it . . . And when they realise, they can't understand. 'You said you loved me.' But you daren't say you didn't because that just proves you're a liar.

JANICE I'd never say that now. Really, you know, it's taught me an awful lot. I feel that going out with that boy for so long has made me very mature in my ideas about love now, and relationships. I learnt a lot from the experience . . . What I really learnt was that the word 'love' is used too loosely. I learnt what to expect from a relationship, and now I'm using what I've learnt with the boy I'm going out with now.

TINA As soon as the word 'love' comes into a relationship, everything starts going haywire.

JANICE People don't realise that you could just go out with somebody, to go out with them, to enjoy their company. But It's never like that. It's always something more complicated. People make things more complicated than what they are. They enjoy doing it.

TINA They try to define relationships when there's no need to.

IN PAIRS

1 Discuss what Paul says about love and obsession at the top of the page. What is the difference?

2 What do you think of Tina's and Janice's views?

● Do you agree with Janice that the word 'love' is used too loosely?

● Do you think that people 'try to define relationships when there's no need to'?

Love is...
...doing things together.

Love not freely given

Love not freely given
Is not given at all.
Love asks nothing,
But asks everything.
Love is understanding.
Love is pain.
Love is the hand that will never leave you,
Yet it is the hand that lets you stand alone.
It is the all seeing eye,
For it sees and hears the heart
It may close its eye
But the heart will know.
It is forgiveness

HOW DO YOU KNOW IF IT'S REALLY LOVE?

Here are some guidelines:
You can't be in love with someone you don't know –
like an actor or pop star. Real love demands real
knowledge.

You can't be in love with someone's lifestyle –
snappy dressing, smart car. It's the person
behind the façade that counts.

You can't be in love with someone just because
your parents think he or she is terrific. It's what
you think that really matters.

You can't be in love with someone if you have to
put on a show for them and hide the real you.

You can't be in love with someone if you're not
prepared to accept them at their worst – like when
they're ill.
Claire Rayner, Womans Own

IN GROUPS

1 What idea of love is given in the poem _Love not freely given_?
Do you agree/disagree with this view of love? Say why.

2 On your own, study this list of qualities that people look for
in a girlfriend/boyfriend and write down the three you think
are the most important.

- Good looks
- Won't let you down
- Consideration
- Hardworking
- Physically fit
- Talented
- Popular
- Looks smart
- Sense of humour
- Good manners
- Not childish
- Has money
- Honesty
- Intelligent

Then, in your group, put the qualities in order of
importance, starting with the most important.

Are there any other qualities which you think are
important but which are not on the list? If so, add them to
your list.

When you have finished, share your ideas in a class
discussion.

3 In pairs look again at all the material on this page and
decide what the word love means to you. Work out a short
definition of love.

Discuss the definitions worked out by your pairs.
Choose the definitions which your group thinks best gives
the idea of what love is.

Then, share your ideas in a class discussion.

Love is...
...taking a stroll together in the evening.

FOR YOUR FOLDER

In pairs discuss what Claire Rayner says about knowing if
you're really in love. Do you agree with her guidelines? Write
down two or three more similar guidelines for your folder.

EXPECTATIONS

What boys say...

'The trouble is, there's all kinds of pressures on you if you ask a girl out. You can't just act natural, just be yourself. You've got to pretend in order to live up to their expectations.'

'Girls expect too much of you. The first time you go out with a girl you're bound to be nervous. But you're not expected to show it. You've got to be quite cool – on top of everything. If you let them see you're scared or mixed up, they'll dump you like a ton of bricks.'

'There's pressures from your friends too. They're always on at you about how far you've gone and what you've done. So you tend to let them think you've done things you haven't, and that can cause all kinds of problems.'

'Everyone tries to hurry you along. Once you start going out with a girl, people start pairing you off. They don't allow you the time and space you need to find out about each other and whether you're really suited. Instead, they start expecting you to do this and do that.'

What girls say...

'The trouble with boys is they expect you to go along with what they want – and most of them only want one thing.'

'The pressures on girls are enormous. It's all right for boys. They can just hang out with their mates. But if you're a girl, you're expected to have a boyfriend. If you don't, there's something wrong with you. And once you've got a boyfriend, you're expected to behave in a stereotyped way. If you don't go along with it, you get a reputation for being "funny".'

'Even in our so-called liberated society there's lots of things a girl's not expected to do: you're not expected to make the first move, you're not expected to draw the line where you want to draw it, you're not expected to stand up to him in front of his mates, whatever he says or does.'

'It's much easier to go out with one of your girlfriends than it is with a boy – there's so much less expected of you. When you're with boys, you're aware they are watching every move you make. You've got to pretend you're sophisticated and grown up, no matter what you're feeling.'

IN GROUPS

- Do boys and girls have to put on an act when they are out together?
- Are there pressures on both girls and boys to behave in a particular way?
- Do girls and boys have particular expectations about each other? Do all boys and all girls share the same expectations?
- What makes boys have certain expectations about girls, and what leads girls to have certain expectations about boys?

FOR YOUR FOLDER

Work with a partner. Write a short play based on the problems that arise because a girl and a boy have different expectations.

What plays a part in your expectations?

- ☐ Friends
- ☐ Books
- ☐ Religion
- ☐ Magazines
- ☐ Advertisements
- ☐ Parents
- ☐ Films
- ☐ Newspapers
- ☐ Televison
- ☐ School
- ☐ Pop Stars/idols
- ☐ Experience

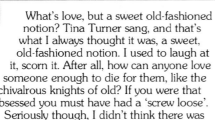

Lover kept his wedding a secret

IN GROUPS

Study the list above of things which might play a part in your expectations, and rate their importance on this scale:
5 stars, extremely important; 4 stars, very important;
3 stars, quite important; 2 stars, not very important; 1 star, only slightly important.

Love and illusions

It is hardly ever questioned whether or not romantic love really exists. Nearly everybody just assumes it does. A partner is still seen as being of vital importance in a person's life. But this should be questioned.

As a working class teenager at a secondary modern school, I went along with my mates in believing in true love and the romantic dream. We avidly read *Jackie* on how to be sexy and pretty, how to get a boyfriend, behave with him, keep him and how, when you fall in love with the right one, it would be for ever (lesbianism was never mentioned). Our world revolved around boys, and life was unthinkable without one – you'd be a failure, not quite a woman. Friends would pity you and arrange blind dates. But most of the lads were revolting. My mother would say, 'Never mind, there's plenty more fish in the sea,' which was no comfort whatsoever.

Although the word love was bandied about carelessly, we all knew precisely what it 'meant': one day we'd meet him, fall in love, and get married. But what a problem, because in reality, you went out with Alec, who could only talk about cars, or John, who was silent, and only wanted snogging sessions. These boys at least paid for us and brought us presents, but if a better one came along, you chucked them. And if they chucked you, you felt it was because you were too spotty, fat, or boring. Or in my case, it was usually because I behaved too clever. You always had to pretend to be thicker than them if you wanted to keep them . . . so slowly I began to realise how impossible the dream of 'Mr Right' was – none of them were gods, they were just as ordinary, weak and stupid as girls were, and I certainly wasn't prepared to pretend to be even more stupid just to please them. It began to seem to me that romantic love was an illusion based on pretending they were something they were not (and pretending you were something else too).

Belinda Yates

Real love?

What's love, but a sweet old-fashioned notion? Tina Turner sang, and that's what I always thought it was, a sweet, old-fashioned notion. I used to laugh at it, scorn it. After all, how can anyone love someone enough to die for them, like the chivalrous knights of old? If you were that obsessed you must have had a 'screw loose'.

Seriously though, I didn't think there was such a head-over-heels-forget-everything-else-love! I mean, most people know the loyal parental love which you feel for your mum and dad.

There's the 'perfect' love too, the temporary crush on the pop star, or actor, or even an older person you know. This person appears to have no faults, because you don't have any actual contact with them.

Small relationships between friends at school are fun. You fancy someone, so you go out with them, have a laugh, have a chat, but then you discover that your new-found friend isn't all you expected. You get bored and so the relationship finishes, but it's nice to think you've both gained something from it.

All the time, you're learning how to handle relationships, what to say, do, how to avoid embarrassment, how to end them and form a friendship. Obviously, there may be some tears somewhere on the line. It's all those little goings on that put you on the right path for 'the real thing'.

You can't go out looking for real love. It finds you. It might hit you in the face and knock you flat, or it might sneak up on you – and you fall in love and into pain, happiness, insecurity, comfort and a whole new feeling of being at one with life. A real love can change your whole outlook on life, give you inspiration where before there was boredom, can make you love where before there was irritation.

Love is a funny human condition. It may be old fashioned, But it'll always be here, so long as we have feelings, and so long as we can be truly happy. Whatever happens, I thoroughly recommend it!
Julie Noble

IN GROUPS

Compare Belinda Yates' views with Julie Noble's. Which of their ideas about love do you share? Which do you disagree with? Say why.

WHY MARRY?

'**I** don't want to get married until I'm about 25. I want to live my life and not get tied down too quickly. I'd expect my husband to do half of the housework. But I'd do the cooking so that I didn't get horrible dinners. I'd do the ironing and the washing too. He could dust and do the hoovering. I wouldn't put up with it if he wouldn't share. I'd get divorced if he wasn't prepared to sort it out.'

Kim

'**I** don't want to get married. My mum divorced when I was three. People have tiffs, they're bound to split up. Some men are just lazy good-for-nothings. I would rather stay with one person and have children when I'm 35. I would take two years off to have children.'

Sandra

Marriage is a partnership between a man and a woman living together. It has been part of most religious beliefs since religions began. Although more people today say that there is no need to marry, there has been no clear sign of a drop in the number of people getting married. However, there has been a drop recently in marriages for young people under 20. In 1984, one in six people who got married was under 20, compared to one in three in 1972.

IN GROUPS

Study the reasons for getting married below. Make a list of the reasons you think are *sensible* for people marrying, even if you don't agree with them yourself. Put this list in order of importance, as agreed by the group. Make a second list of reasons why people should *not* get married and put it into order of importance as well.

CLASS DISCUSSION

Study the most important reasons for and against getting married. Discuss the similarities and differences.

FOR YOUR FOLDER

Make a note of the reasons given for and against marriage that you find the most important. Write a short statement, similar to Kim's and Sandra's, saying how you feel about marriage.

REASONS FOR GETTING MARRIED

Our religion stresses the need for marriage if we want to live together.

We don't want our children to be illegitimate.

Pressure from friends and relatives.

It gives extra strength to our relationship.

When we simply lived together, it caused all sorts of embarrassment.

To get away from home.

It's easier to buy or rent a house if you are married.

Marriage is the accepted and normal step for people in love.

It provides a stable family life in which our children can grow up.

We were expecting a baby and so we decided we had better get married.

We found we would be financially better off married than living together.

Ours was an arranged marriage as this is what our religion requires.

I wanted to make certain that I had a legal share of my partner's money.

We had to get married so that my partner could stay in the country.

Teenage marriages

JANE and BOB

Jane was 17 and I was 19 when we were married. It turned out to be a complete disaster. We thought we loved each other but once the problems started to build up, and our passion started to decrease, our relationship could not stand the strain.

Our lack of understanding about the demands of marriage and our own immaturity meant the marriage never stood a chance.

I suppose that if we had really loved each other we could have overcome the problems of building a home: the bills, the restrictions of bringing up children, cooking, cleaning, decorating and all the other everyday things that go with living together.

I doubt now that we ever loved each other, but if we did we were both still changing and developing so much that we eventually grew apart.

It is more likely that we confused the emotions of sexual attraction with love. Once these started to decrease we both began to find fault with each other.

Eventually we both realised that we had made a mistake getting married as early as we did and agreed to a divorce. It was not a pleasant experience. Never think of divorce as the easy way out of this kind of mistake. It's not!

TREVOR and JILL

When Trevor and I got married we were both 18 years old. Although we have had our ups and downs, like most marriages, we are very happy together.

We didn't have children straight away. We decided to wait a few years so that we could go out with our friends enjoy ourselves without the restrictions that a baby places on you.

During our first years of marriage we got to know each other as only married couples can; good points and bad. Once we had built a home based on a firm relationship we decided to have children. The beauty of getting married so early is that we are still young enough to take a full and active part as our children grow up. Also, once they become independent, we will still be young enough to go out and enjoy ourselves all over again.

I am glad we decided to get married so young. It allowed our relationship to develop much more quickly than it would have done had we both still been living with our parents. We could learn and develop together and I am sure that this has strengthened our love.

It takes effort and patience to overcome the inevitable problems in any marriage; probably more so if you are young. If you love each other, however, you can solve these problems no matter whether you marry at 18 or 80.

IN GROUPS

Bob said, 'It is more likely that we confused the emotions of sexual attraction with love.'
What do you think he meant?

Bob mentioned developing, changing and growing apart. What do you think he meant by this?

Jill, on the other hand, mentioned learning and developing together. What do you think she meant by this?

What do you think is the main reason that Jane and Bob's marriage failed, but Trevor and Jill's marriage succeeded?

Based on the stories and ideas from the group, make a list of the advantages and disadvantages of teenage marriages. Share your list with the other groups.

FOR YOUR FOLDER

Teenage marriages are more likely to end in divorce than marriages where the partners are older. Does this surprise you? Give your reasons.

HOMOSEXUALITY

Some people prefer to have a relationship with members of their own sex – that is, they are homosexual. Surveys show that about one person in ten is gay.

Society, however, is geared towards male and female coupling, or heterosexuality. Homosexuality is often looked upon as abnormal (although it is no longer treated as a crime in the United Kingdom if the partners are 21 years of age or over). This means that gay teenagers often have great pressures on them. For, in addition to the usual problems people have in learning to form relationships, homosexuals may face prejudice, disapproval and rejection.

More and more homosexuals are open and active in trying to gain rights and acceptance. There are also groups for teenagers which help young people learn more about homosexuality and their own feelings about it.

SEX BEFORE MARRIAGE?

"What's so immoral about showing your feelings towards your partner in a sexual way?" she says. "Surely, having sex with someone you love is the most natural thing in the world. The first boy you have sex with might not be the one you end up marrying, but I don't think that makes having sex with that person 'wrong'. Sex with someone you're very close to is a very special thing, whether you're married or not, and I don't believe that the fact that you're not married necessarily cheapens the act of making love. Obviously, you must take precautions, and it's important to discuss this beforehand.

"I think you always know when the time's right for you to have sex for the very first time. You can't say, 'Right, now I'm 16 I'll do it' or, 'I know I won't have sex until I'm married,' because everyone matures at different ages. I wouldn't say that a girl was wrong to have sex at 16, in the same way that it's perfectly OK to be a virgin at 20.

"The sexual side of my relationship is very important to me. It's simply a way of showing my love for my boyfriend, and although a relationship consists of more than just sex, I know I'd find it difficult to have a fulfilling relationship without it."

Nicola, 19

'Never do anything you don't want to do. Never let anyone pressure you into behaviour or actions you're not ready for, anything that doesn't feel right for you, whether it's sexual or not.'

Judy Blume in *Letters to Judy*

It's your choice

YES or NO

"I'm a Christian," she says, "and I've been brought up in a Christian home. I've grown up to believe that sex before marriage is wrong – but even if it wasn't for my religion, I'd still have my morals. That's just me, I suppose. It's part of my character. I just don't see the point in having sex before you're married.

"Of course, I can have normal relationships with boys without having sex with them. I met Paul, my boyfriend, when the young people from the churches in our area went away for a weekend. We've been going out together for four months and luckily we share the same beliefs. Sex just doesn't matter to us. We've discussed it, we've agreed that we don't want to have sex and it doesn't cause any problems at all. If anything, I think sex can *cause* problems between couples. A girl might have sex only because she's afraid she'll lose her boyfriend if she doesn't. Then, once you'd had sex, you'll have it again and again. It's never just a one-off thing – that's the problem of saying yes.

"If anything, I think Paul and I talk to each other more than couples who have sex are likely to. Besides, there are other ways of expressing your love: you can say 'I love you' or give your boyfriend a massive cuddle. A boy might say, 'If you love me, you'll have sex with me,' but I'd reply, 'If you love me, you *won't* have sex with me.' I'd be livid if a boy tried to blackmail me into having sex with him and I'd think: so you had one aim all along. To get me into bed. I'd be so disappointed. I know I'll never give in to demands like that. When you really love someone, you don't need to prove it that way.

Jane, 17

CONTRACEPTION

the sheath, or diaphragm or cap with spermicide

If you are going to have any sexual relationship and don't want to have a baby it is essential that you use a reliable form of contraception. If you are over 16 you can get confidential advice about contraception from your GP or a Family Planning Clinic.

IN GROUPS

How do you feel about sex before marriage?
Discuss Nicola's view and Jane's view. Pick out the points in their statements that you agree with and that you disagree with. Say why. Would you expect boys to present different arguments either for or against sex before marriage? Why?

FOR YOUR FOLDER

Write out a statement giving your views about sex before marriage.

SEXUALLY TRANSMITTED DISEASES

If you decide to have a very active sex life, there are risks. You might get pregnant, or you might catch a sexually transmitted disease – VD or AIDS. No cure has yet been found for AIDS. Doctors believe that many people with the disease will eventually die from it.

The safest ways to protect yourself are not to have sexual relationships or to stick to one partner. The more sexual partners you have, the more likely you are to catch a sexually transmitted disease. The use of a condom (sometimes called 'safe sex') reduces the dangers but does not give full protection.

IN GROUPS

Do you think the government's campaign to inform people about AIDS is working?

Do you think the fear of AIDS has changed people's feelings about sex? Has it changed their sexual activity? Has it changed your attitude towards casual sex?

QUESTION BOX

Are there any questions you want answered about AIDS?

Ask your teacher to supply a question box to hold questions class members drop in – without names, of course. Ask her to arrange an answering session too.

IN GROUPS

Read the article *Buddy can you spare the time* and discuss what qualities you think someone would need in order to be a 'Buddy' for a person with AIDS.

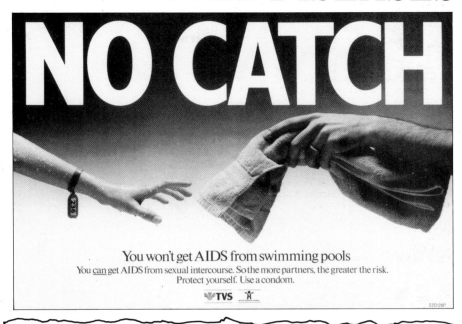

You won't get AIDS from swimming pools
You <u>can</u> get AIDS from sexual intercourse. So the more partners, the greater the risk.
Protect yourself. Use a condom.

TVS

STD-28P

Buddy can you spare the time?

Terrence Higgins was the first person in this country to die of AIDS. That was in 1982. His friends set up a charity – The Terence Higgins Trust – to help with what they saw as a major impending crisis. The Trust now has 350 volunteer workers. 150 of them "buddies". Buddies – volunteers – visit sick people with AIDS (PWAs).

The business of buddying is the thing the Trust does which is least like what any other organisation does. It seems particularly hard for outsiders even to image. When the American film *Buddies* was shown on Channel 4 recently, it started a rush of inquiries from possible volunteers, who perhaps hadn't considered buddying before. In the film, the sick man is in hospital, and has no human contacts except with the nursing staff until the buddy comes along. But it isn't always like that. In fact there's so much variety that training becomes almost irrelevant. It can't prepare you for everything. So sooner or later you'll have to fall back on your own resources.

You can talk to your PWA about the future of the illness, the disappointment it has in store. Point out that what is likely to happen first is not a cure, nor even a vaccine, but a holding pattern, as insulin is a holding pattern for diabetes.

You may, of course, do some talking about death. You may visit your PWA on a day when he's having trouble getting his words out, but he's written a little list of things he wants to talk about. On the pad are the words "Mass", "He Min" and "Fun". It takes a little coaxing before he remembers what they mean. He's ashamed of his bad handwriting, and he forgets the words. "Mass" turns out to be "massage", which he wants because his buttocks and upper legs are sore from just sitting around. "He Min" is the Health Minister. Your PWA is brewing a letter. And "Fun" means funeral, about which he has definite ideas. His parents and his lover both try to shut him up when he raises the subject, so he's telling you, and he'd like you to type up three copies of instructions please, just to be on the safe side.

You may end up embracing those same parents late one night in the hospital, and wondering when is the tactful moment to hand over the piece of paper with the details about the plywood and the posies. And they may thank you, say what would they have done without you, and then say they hope you come to the service, but could you please not mention the cause of death.

WORKING ON YOUR OWN

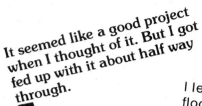

It seemed like a good project when I thought of it. But I got fed up with it about half way through.

I left my notes lying on the floor. Then my mum came in and tidied up and I couldn't find some of them.

I did the research a fortnight before writing up the project. So I couldn't remember everything I'd found out.

I spent ages doing the research, so I didn't have any time left to do the write up. I had to do it in a rush to get it in on time.

COURSEWORK PROBLEMS

The trouble is, I've got two coursework projects due in at the same time. I'm getting behind with the rest of my schoolwork.

I got fed up with the research. I couldn't seem to find the information I wanted. So I copied it all out of this book I found.

It's all very well teachers giving us detailed advice on how to do our coursework projects, but how can you fit it all in? There's so much else going on. I play hockey every Saturday and there's practice twice a week. By the time I've done my chores and my babysitting, there's no time left.

I tried doing mine on a word processor and then lost most of it because I touched the wrong key!

IN PAIRS

Talk about the problems each of these eight students are having. Write down what advice you would give each of them. Then, join up with another pair and compare your advice.

IN GROUPS

Study the advice taken from a guide to coursework on the next page. On your own, list the three pieces of advice you think are the most useful. Then, in your groups, take it in turns to explain why you think so.

COURSEWORK GUIDELINES

How should I go about writing my research?

Collect information bit by bit and be ready to change your plans if what you are finding points in a different direction. Don't leave things until the last minute.

Don't attempt to write up your project as you go along. You will not be able to see how everything fits together until you have all the information.

Keep a diary of your research in a small notebook. Jot down everything that happens during your research, like what letters you write, what books you look at, how you feel the research is going, and so on. Write down the date of each entry in your diary.

Remember that everything that happens during your research is important to it – people who don't help you or who write silly things on questionnaires, organisations that don't reply to your letters. Writing about these things will show the examiner that you have faced the same problems that all researchers do, and that you know a problem when you meet one.

Write up any work you do as soon as you can after having completed it. If you leave it any length of time you might forget what happened.

Look after your notes very carefully; try to get a file you can keep all your coursework material in.

Be prepared to go through different moods while doing your coursework; sometimes you may feel cheerful and full of enthusiasm for the project; other times you may feel bored and unwilling to work at it. Hopefully, the let-down mood will not last long.

Eventually you should have lots of bits of written information, called 'field notes' – this is all the data you have collected as well as notes on how the research went. Now you can begin to plan the final form of your research project.

How should I present my research project?

Plan your research project before you begin to write it. Draw up a list of headings in the order you intend to follow.

Write your own project in rough first. Correct this rough and make a neat final copy.

Make your coursework look as attractive as possible with visual material such as graphs, diagrams, pictures, cartoons, newspaper and magazine articles. Why not take some photographs yourself and include them? Remember to label clearly all visual material.

Make sure whatever you include is to the point. Don't be afraid to leave material out if it does not add anything to your project.

You should include an appendix at the end. This is a section for many sorts of material, such as examples of questionnaires, interview schedules, a list of books you used, organisations you wrote to, places you visited, your research diary, and other field notes. Include all of these if possible.

Don't number the pages until you are sure that you won't be changing anything before you hand it in. Remember, you can't make a table of contents until all the pages are correctly numbered.

Check list

Your coursework should usually include:

1 Why you chose the topic you did
2 Why you chose the aims or basic idea you did
3 Why you chose the research methods you did
4 How you did the research
5 The problems you had doing the research
6 Your findings and how you interpret them
7 Your conclusions, including what you have discovered about your basic idea or the general aims of your research
8 What changes you would make if you repeated the research
9 What further research might be useful to make your project better
10 An appendix

GETTING DOWN TO WORK

How easy do you find it to get down to work? The way you go about your studies can either help you or hold you back. It's important to understand what you feel helps pupils do well at school.

Beliefs about doing well at school

1 Pupils who do well in tests usually get a lot of help from their parents.

2 Teachers only praise you to make you work harder.

3 When you fail it is usually because you did not work hard enough.

4 Regular study usually leads to good results.

5 You should see how you get on in your GCSE examinations before you plan what to do next.

6 When you get things wrong it is because the teacher did not explain it clearly.

7 If you are told you don't have the ability there is no point in trying.

8 Doing well in exams seems to be a matter of luck.

9 At our age it is difficult to study because you have to go out with friends.

10 I usually seem to do badly when I have to compete with others.

11 Pupils usually say the exam was unfair when they haven't prepared for it.

12 There is not much point in trying to do well if you are not sure you can get a good job when you leave school.

13 Doing well in a subject depends on whether or not you like the teacher.

14 You can learn from your mistakes how to do better next time.

15 Doing badly in exams usually means that the pupil was not taught properly.

WORKING

I'm expected to stay in my room all evening. If I so much as go downstairs to make myself a cup of coffee, There's a great inquest about it.

I'm fed up with the way they keep comparing me to my sister Susan. They expect me to be like her and work all the time. It's unfair the way they force me to stay at my studies. It makes me so angry I can't concentrate properly when I do try to work.

We've had lots of rows lately about the amount of time I spend out with my friends. Why can't they leave me alone and let me organise my own life? It's up to me what I do with it.

ON YOUR OWN

Study the list of beliefs about doing well at school. Divide a piece of paper into three columns headed: Agree, Disagree, Uncertain. Put each statement into the column you decide upon. Beneath each statement, write your reasons for your decision.

IN GROUPS

Take each statement one by one. Discuss which column each of you put it in, and say why.

T HOME

I like having the TV on while I'm working, but my dad goes mad when he sees me. He switches it off and yells at me. He's sure I can't work with the TV on.

It's not easy to study in our house. How can I concentrate with my two brothers tearing about the house all the time? I've asked my parents to speak to them about it, but it doesn't make any difference.

You can't work all the time can you? But if I'm on the phone for more than five minutes they jump on me: 'Don't spend all your time gossiping on the phone. Your exams are coming up, you know!' It gets me down.

Unsuccessful students

1 Need outside controls, such as rewards and praise, from parents and teachers.

2 Do not try to measure their own work, but depend on the teacher's comments to find out how they are doing.

3 Work only sufficiently to get by with what parents, teachers and examiners ask for.

4 Believe that luck is what matters in life.

5 Blame other people for their problems, including failing.

6 Look to parents and teachers to tell them what they should aim for at school and in life.

7 More often than not, copy out ideas of others without thinking about them.

Successful students

1 Get their rewards from meeting the high standards they set for themselves.

2 Look for ways of reaching their study goals.

3 See that the subjects they are studying are important to their plans for the future.

4 Blame no one but themselves for failures, but also recognise their success.

5 Keep at it when problems arise, looking for ways to improve or change their study methods.

6 Try different, new ways of studying and of solving their problems, relying largely on themselves.

IN GROUPS

1 Discuss the kind of problems you face when trying to get down to work at home. Suggest ways of trying to cope with these difficulties.
   Prepare a group statement about the difficulties of studying at home, and how to deal with them. Then share your ideas in a class discussion.

2 Study the notes at the top of this page. Discuss what they tell you about how the unsuccessful students and the successful students differ in their attitudes.

ROLE PLAY

IN PAIRS

Choose one of the teenager's statements about working at home. Discuss what you think their parent(s) would say. Act out a scene in which the teenager and one parent discuss studying. Do the scene twice. The first time, make it end in a row. The second time, have it lead to a calm discussion in which each listens to the other's point of view.

What are YOU

Here are 25 acts or situations which you must judge in terms of being wrong, using a scale of 1 to 10. You choose 1 if the item seems not wrong at all or least wrong, and choose 10 if you think the item is completely wrong or most wrong. Use the numbers 2 to 9 for the in-between levels of wrongness. List the numbers 1 – 25 and write your choice against each number. For example if you think number 1 is most wrong write: 1 – 10.

Least wrong ⟶ **Most wrong**

1	Sniffing glue to get high	1	2	3	4	5	6	7	8	9	10
2	Failing to keep promises very often	1	2	3	4	5	6	7	8	9	10
3	Smoking marijuana at a party	1	2	3	4	5	6	7	8	9	10
4	An asbestos factory not changing working conditions known to be dangerous to the workers' health	1	2	3	4	5	6	7	8	9	10
5	Doctors allowing a badly deformed baby to die when its life could be saved	1	2	3	4	5	6	7	8	9	10
6	An MP working for the passage of a law known to be against the public interest, because they will make money out of it	1	2	3	4	5	6	7	8	9	10
7	Having affairs while married	1	2	3	4	5	6	7	8	9	10
8	A nation dealing unjustly with a weaker nation over which it has power	1	2	3	4	5	6	7	8	9	10
9	Living beyond your means in order to possess luxuries other people have	1	2	3	4	5	6	7	8	9	10
10	Not voting during national elections	1	2	3	4	5	6	7	8	9	10
11	Euthanasia (causing the death of another person painlessly to end their suffering) as a way of dealing with someone having an incurable illness.	1	2	3	4	5	6	7	8	9	10
12	Copying from another person's paper in an exam	1	2	3	4	5	6	7	8	9	10
13	Getting a divorce when both partners agree that they just can't get along	1	2	3	4	5	6	7	8	9	10
14	Lying about qualifications in a job interview	1	2	3	4	5	6	7	8	9	10
15	Taking your own life in a case where there are no near relatives or dependants	1	2	3	4	5	6	7	8	9	10
16	Using offensive language in mixed company	1	2	3	4	5	6	7	8	9	10

moral values?

17	Using the cane at school to punish misbehaving children.	1	2	3	4	5	6	7	8	9	10
18	Using science to produce a highly intelligent test-tube baby	1	2	3	4	5	6	7	8	9	10
19	Allowing yourself to be conscripted to fight in a war you believe is unjust	1	2	3	4	5	6	7	8	9	10
20	Advertising, and then selling a medicine to cure a disease, although this medicine cannot do so	1	2	3	4	5	6	7	8	9	10
21	Accepting money for your vote in small local elections	1	2	3	4	5	6	7	8	9	10
22	Newspapers treating crime news so as to make criminals seem like heroes	1	2	3	4	5	6	7	8	9	10
23	A nation at war using napalm on the cities of its enemy	1	2	3	4	5	6	7	8	9	10
24	A 14-year-old girl taking the contraceptive pill	1	2	3	4	5	6	7	8	9	10
25	A man not marrying the girl he wants to marry because she comes from a lower class and has less education	1	2	3	4	5	6	7	8	9	10

Scoring

The test covers five different categories: Basic morality, Family morality, Social morality, Community morality and Political morality. Copy the score chart on the right. You will see the items, by number, which come under each category. On your copy write in the score you gave the item, then add up each score column and write in the total score. Form groups and compare your views.

Comparing your scores on the different categories will show where your strongest feelings lie.

High score 35-50: very strong feelings

17-34: average feelings

Low score 1-16: very weak feelings.

Basic morality

ITEMS SCORE

2 _____
5 _____
11 _____   Total
12 _____
15 _____

Family morality

ITEMS SCORE

7 _____
13 _____
17 _____   Total
18 _____
24 _____

Social morality

ITEMS SCORE

4 _____
8 _____
14 _____   Total
20 _____
22 _____

Community morality

ITEMS SCORE

1 _____
3 _____
9 _____   Total
16 _____
25 _____

Political morality

ITEMS SCORE

6 _____
10 _____
19 _____   Total
21 _____
23 _____

Remember that morality is cultural, and varies from one society to another, and from one period of time to another.

FOR YOUR FOLDER

Choose one of the items for which you gave a high score, showing that you feel very strongly about it as a moral issue. Write a statement explaining why you feel this way.

Do you believe in God?

And if you do what difference does it make to your life?
Six people talk about their religious beliefs.

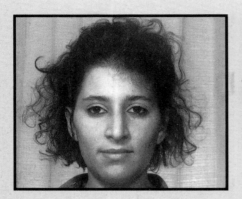

Judaism

**Simone Berg, 17
from Liverpool**

I've had a religious upbringing; since the age of four I've attended a Jewish school and so Judaism is a major part of my life.

'In the Jewish religion, The Sabbath (Friday night and Saturday) is the most important part of the week. I've never been allowed to go out on a Friday night, but I've honestly never wanted to. On Friday night all the family get together and have a small service, light candles and eat a special meal. It's lovely and there's a strong sense of togetherness in the family.

'I've always believed in God. It gives me a purpose for being here, but I believe more than I practise. We keep a kosher home (that means all the meat in our house is killed in a special way) and we observe other Jewish dietary laws such as keeping milk and meat products separate and not eating pork.

'I've never doubted God, but I do occasionally question the Old Testament. I wouldn't marry someone who wasn't Jewish. I don't think I'd be happy with a man who didn't share my faith and traditions. I wouldn't feel secure and have peace of mind. I need faith to go on.'

Islam

**Shaheen Pathan, 21
from London**

'My mother is a strict Moslem, keeping up with the Moslem culture at home and praying regularly, but for me and my six sisters it just isn't practical. At work and school, we can't put a mat on the floor and start praying five times a day; and when I used to wear traditional Moslem costume in the street I got a lot of abuse. As Moslems living in a Western society we *have* to adapt.

'In the Koran (our Bible) men and women are equal, but in practice it's a different matter. Boys are encouraged to have a career, but as soon as a girl has completed her A levels she's expected to 'settle down'.

'I believe in God, but I never pray. I do, however, stick to religious days and customs like Ramadan, where for a month we fast completely from sunrise to sunset (about 18 hours). It makes you clean inside, and is meant to make you feel sympathetic towards the poor.

'I believe there is a God, but I don't believe he's done anything for us yet.'

Rastafarianism

**Gladstone Catwell, 17
from Sheffield**

'Rastafarianism is a way of life rather than a religion. I don't go to a church to pray. I pray at home and, at certain times of the year – for example on the birthday of his imperial majesty Haile Selassie (our Christmas) – we have gatherings and we talk and reason and interpret the Bible, bouncing ideas around and trying to understand the verses and how they affect us today. I believe God created man and woman and gave us a part of himself – the soul. Therefore God is in all of us. Men *and* women both play an important part in life. We can't fulfil our purpose alone.

'My faith has calmed me down a lot – although I'm still learning about the religion (it takes about five years to acquire the knowledge).

'I wear the Rasta colours – green for the earth, gold for the African sun, and red for the blood of the people. This also links us with Africa as these are the colours of the Ethiopian flag. The dreadlocks come from the Old Testament which says you shouldn't put a razor to your head or face. The modern interpretation is that we don't use a comb either. I used to have locks, but they were ripped out by the police and by my brother who is a Christian and resents me being a Rastafarian. From our appearance we look militant, but inside we're peace-loving people.'

Each choose one of the six statements below, which interests you, either because you share the religious beliefs of the person or because you learned something new about their religion from what they said. Read the statement again. Then take it in turns to tell the rest of the group about the writer's beliefs and why you find them interesting.

Work on your own and write a statement about your own religious beliefs, or lack of them, to put in your folder. Then, form groups and read and discuss your statements.

Christianity

**Katharine Maines, 18
from Porthcawl**

'A lot of young people get dis-illusioned with the Church because it appears hypocritical. Sometimes I sit in church, bored and restless, and I think, What's the point in all this? For me, the answer is never far away – It's because Christianity is exciting and challenging. Corny as it sounds, it's a *joyful* thing.

'I go to church twice on Sundays, and during the week if it's a special occasion. I also try to set aside time, usually no more than five minutes, each day to pray. I tend to divide my prayer into sections. I spend some time being thankful for what I've got, some time apologising for things I've done and some time praying for others and their needs.

'I also think part of Christian commitment is to make an effort to do some sort of service to the community. If I see someone in need I try to help them rather than ignore the situation. If someone seems lonely, I'll try to talk to them and I also help run holiday camps for the physically handicapped. Yes, as a Christian I strive to be good, but nobody's perfect.'

Catholicism

**John Egan, 16
from Leeds**

'I pray every day; not in a conventional kneel-down-and-bow-your-head way. I talk to God when I'm on bus or walking along.

'I'm not pressurised by my parents. The choice to be a practising Catholic (rather than one in name only) is mine. I go to mass every Sunday and sing in the choir. We take communion and as a Cathloic, I believe transubstantiation takes place – this means I truly believe that the bread and wine we eat become the body and blood of Christ, just as it did at the Last Supper.

'I go to confession about ten times a year. Speaking to God through the priest, I discuss my problems and sins and then the priest gives absolution and gives me a penance, usually something like saying three Hail Marys and a sacrifice like missing my favourite TV programme. I don't have to do these things, but I feel obliged morally.

'Believing in God gives me a sense of purpose. It'd be so depressing to think that when you die you just stay in the ground. If that's the case, then life is pointless. I believe in heaven and hell; not in angels and fire; to me heaven is with God and hell is without God.'

Atheism

**Lindsey Hilton, 22
from London**

'I wish I could tell you exactly why I don't believe in God, but it's a feeling rather than an informed theory. I've always been a cynical person with my feet planted firmly on the ground, and I need proof for everything.

'The Bible, for example, is like Aesop's Fables – where's the evidence? The idea that when I die my soul lives on and even goes to heaven would be most comforting, but again, where's the evidence?

'In a world full of suffering and hopelessness, the belief that a God is watching over us and guiding everybody seems to me a paradox. As far as I can see, there's no salvation for righteousnesss and likewise no eternal damnation for being evil. I believe that people create their own destiny; that they get out of life just what they put in – be it good or bad. A God doesn't direct our lives.

'It seems to me that many people use religion as a crutch, a security blanket. They don't question their faith because without it they see no point in us being here, it's just too bleak a prospect. However, I don't knock people with faith. Everybody is entitled to their own beliefs. If religion is part of someone's life, that's fine – but it's not for me.'

PLANNING A BUDGET

Your first regular income

To someone who has been used to pocket money or a Saturday job, the pleasure of that first payment, all your own, is enormous. For many, it is the first time that such a large sum of money has been in their hands, especially on a regular basis.

But unfortunately, that feeling doesn't last long. What seems so huge in one lump sum soon dribbles away in the expense of just living. It can be very tempting to blow much of that money on a couple of items, while you're feeling flush, but then life has a nasty habit of reminding you of its existence by piling on the costs — midday meals, travel to and from work, a new pair of shoes. Money has to last, and the first step to achieving that is through a budget.

There are people who thoroughly enjoy the process of organising a budget. For many it is a bore and a nuisance. However you feel about it, there are definite advantages to working out how much money you have and how much money you can spend. There's a great deal of pleasure in realising at the end of the week that there will be a certain amount of money left over — to play with or save, as you wish.

How much do I spend?

It doesn't make sense to get down to planning future spending before you have some idea of how you spend the money right now. You may not spend the money the same way tomorrow as yesterday, but at least it will give you some guide.

One useful tip is, for six or eight weeks, to record in a notebook every bit of money spent — even down to the last icecream and daily paper. That way you'll get a good idea of where the money goes — and where to stop it going. Don't choose an unrepresentative time of year — holiday or pre-Christmas.

Working out where it goes

Your spending will fall into main areas, such as:

☐ Everyday expenses — food, travel, newspapers

☐ Regular outgoings — paying your parents for your keep or, if you leave home, rent, electricity and gas bills, season tickets.

☐ Irregular items — holidays, treats etc.

☐ Unpredictable expenses — for emergencies. You can't really budget for them but should have something in reserve.

Wise spending

Travel

If you enjoyed reduced rates while travelling to school, prices of local travel might come as rather a shock. But there are ways of making it cheaper, like travelcards or season tickets. There are a range of rail cards and reductions for young people. And long-distance coaches can be very cheap.

Tempting though it may be to own a car, you have to bear in mind the cost of running a car with tax, insurance, petrol, MOT's and garage bills. Remember, a bicycle keeps you fit and bike riders will tell you that it doesn't rain as often as car drivers think it does.

Food shopping

One of the most tedious tasks is having to do your own shopping. It can become an expensive chore unless you make a clear list beforehand, and stick to it. It can be easier at the corner shop, especially when you run out of something at inconvenient times, although the prices tend to be a little higher. The best way to take advantage of supermarkets is to go for special offers. Don't make the mistake of buying masses of something if you don't know for certain that you like it. Go for the supermarkets "Own Brand", often made by the same companies as the named brands. Avoid ready-made meals.

Remember that fruit and vegetables are often cheaper on the market stalls outside, particularly if you go at the end of the day.

Don't assume that you have to eat a lot of meat to eat well. Many tasty vegetarian dishes are cheaper.

Household goods

Research your purchases before you make them. Your local library will probably stock copies of the WHICH? monthly consumer guides. These give regular surveys of almost everything you can buy, with information and advice on the best buys. Don't always assume that the places that look cheapest sell the cheapest goods.

Try comparing the prices of discount warehouses with those of the local department store. Sometimes the price is very little different and if you are buying an important piece of equipment, like a stereo, it is worth knowing that if it goes wrong you can take it back and get an exchange. Many department stores and chain stores will do this, whereas some shops may just take the faulty goods and return them to the manufacturer, leaving you without their use until a replacement arrives.

Look at the small ads in the local papers. Often you find perfectly decent stuff being sold secondhand for very reasonable prices — but make sure it's in working order. Auctions are good and exciting places to pick up bargains if you are careful — and if you control yourself. Instead of buying videos, cassettes and records, consider hiring them from your library.

CLOTHES

On the whole, life is a lot cheaper if you are not fashion-conscious. Look around for some of the presentable nearly-new shops and don't turn your nose up at Oxfam shops either, especially in the well-heeled areas. Jumble sales, too, in such areas can yield treasures, but you'll have to queue.

Army surplus and camping shops are worth a look for pullovers, shirts and jeans.

Try mail order catalogues. There are a number of smaller and more specialist catalogues, some of which offer budget terms.

Look out for special offers in Sunday colour supplements and magazines.

Don't buy clothes that have to be dry cleaned.

Here are two examples of budgets of people in their first jobs

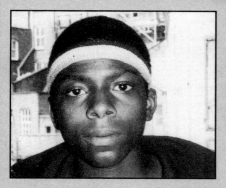

TERRY MOLYNEUX left school at 16, determined to start work at the first opportunity. He was sent by the youth careers office to Bulldog Cases, a small firm in North London making protective flight cases mainly for the music industry, where he began a six-month Youth Opportunities Scheme.

When his training finished, Terry returned to the Careers Office. "They sent me back to Bulldog for a second six-month scheme. I was surprised, but pleased.

"After that scheme had finished, I started working permanently," said Terry. This meant a large increase in weekly take-home pay from £26.50 to £39.50, which has since risen.

His social life is fairly conservative. He doesn't drink but spends most of his cash on "clothes, records and going out". He also hands over £10 a week to his mother to help her with the bills for their Camden Town home. The other regular expenditure is on bus and tube fares to work and to the club where Terry plays hockey every weekend.

SARAH BANHAM is an 18 year old trainee clerical officer at County Hall in Chester who lives with her parents in Hooton, a small town about ten miles from her office.

She gets a lift to work with a colleague but once a week she attends a local college where she studies by day release for her BEC conversion exams.

As with many government jobs, there are regular pay rises. She has just received an increment on her 18th birthday, and will get another if she passes her exams. This latest rise prompted her to join a union: NALGO (National Association of Local Government Officers). Her training finishes in July, when she will have a certain amount of choice about which department to move into.

Although Sarah drives, she hasn't taken the plunge into car ownership. "I'll wait until I can afford it. It can be quite expensive!"

In the meantime, she is able to save towards a holiday in Greece and have the occasional night out or shop in Chester or Liverpool.

Terry's weekly budget

Income (after deductions)		£45.00
Outgoings: Hi-Fi payments		
(to employers)	£ 5.00	
Housekeeping	£10.00	
Travelling	£ 7.00	
Clothes/records	£10.00	
Entertainment	£10.00	
Cigarettes	£ 3.00	
Total	**£45.00**	

Sarah's weekly budget

Income (after deductions)		£60.00
Outgoings: Housekeeping		
to Mum	£12.50	
Savings for hols./car	£20.00	
College/work		
expenses	£ 7.50	
Entertainment	£10.00	
Clothes etc.	£10.00	
Total	**£60.00**	

A PLACE OF YOUR OWN

Leaving home

Most young people leave home between the ages of 16 and 25. There are many reasons for leaving home. Here are several of the many different reasons for leaving home. How acceptable or unacceptable do you think the different reasons are for young people and their families?

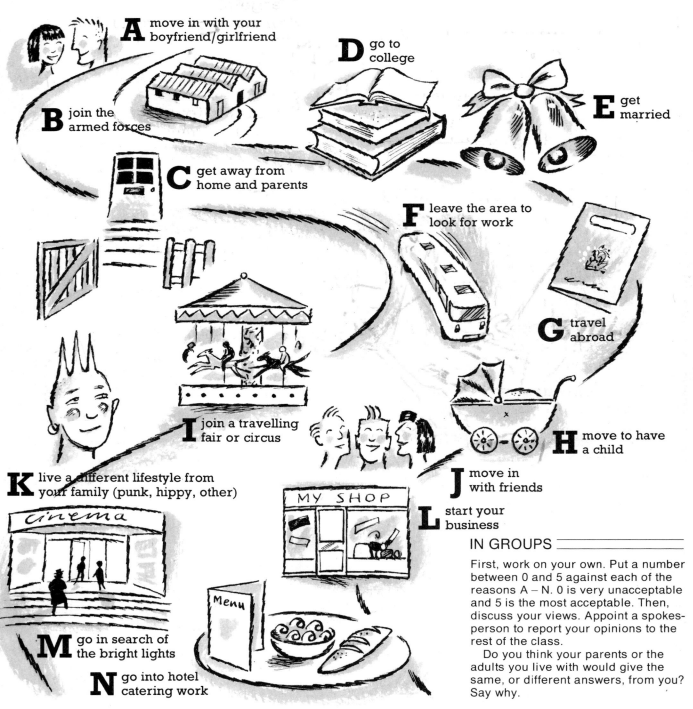

A move in with your boyfriend/girlfriend

B join the armed forces

C get away from home and parents

D go to college

E get married

F leave the area to look for work

G travel abroad

H move to have a child

I join a travelling fair or circus

J move in with friends

K live a different lifestyle from your family (punk, hippy, other)

L start your business

M go in search of the bright lights

N go into hotel catering work

IN GROUPS

First, work on your own. Put a number between 0 and 5 against each of the reasons A – N. 0 is very unacceptable and 5 is the most acceptable. Then, discuss your views. Appoint a spokesperson to report your opinions to the rest of the class.

Do you think your parents or the adults you live with would give the same, or different answers, from you? Say why.

Needs and expectations

1 Where are you living at the moment? Are you happy living there?

2 If you are still living at home, when do you plan to leave? Why? What are your parents' views?

3 How difficult do you think it will be to leave? How would you manage on your own in strange surroundings?

4 Do you think it would be easier if you left to go to college or to live with someone else?

5 How easy do you think it will be to find somewhere to live?

6 What sort of place would you like to live in?

7 What sort of price do you think you will have to pay for somewhere to live? Can you afford it? What do you think is 'reasonable'?

8 Have you considered the following:
   a) Would you like to live alone or share?
   b) Would you want to share a bathroom or kitchen with strangers?
   c) How much space would you like?
   d) Would you like a garden?
   e) Would you like to keep pets?
   f) Would you like to be near friends and family?
   g) Would you prefer to be near shops, transport, place of work or study?

9 How great is the difference between your 'ideal home' and where you think you might end up living?

10 How long would you like to live in one place?

11 Would you prefer to buy or to rent? What do you think you'll end up doing? If you want to buy, what sort of difficulties do you anticipate?

IN GROUPS

Use the questions above to find out about your own needs and expectations. Then produce a statement saying what you have learned from the discussion about the various wants and needs of the people in your group. Say how easy or difficult you think it will be to meet them. Share your statements in a class discussion.

Somewhere to live

Council housing   Most young people who leave home have to find private rented accommodation. You may be able to get into council housing, but in many areas there are long waiting lists. If you are young and single, you may find that you have to wait before you can even put your name down on the council house waiting list.

Lodgings   Usually a room in a family home, with some meals cooked for you. You have to share a bathroom and toilet. Sometimes you are able to use the sitting room.

Bedsit   You get a room of your own, which is set up as both bedroom and sitting room. You will either have a small cooker or share a kitchen. You have to share a bathroom and toilet. The owner or manager may live in the building.

Flat   You get one or more rooms as well as a kitchen, bathroom and toilet. Flats are more expensive and often hard to find. You may have to share with people you do not know, including sharing a bedroom. You have to help look after the flat and share the payment of bills, such as electricity and gas. The landlord often does not live on the premises.

Hostel   You may get either a room or a flat in this special sort of accommodation. Usually you have to share bathrooms and toilets. There may be a kitchen or meals may be provided. You do not have to pay for heating, lighting and hot water, and there may be a laundry room and a TV room. You may have to share a room. There will be rules you have to keep.

IN GROUPS

Discuss each type of accommodation in turn and list its advantages and disadvantages. List the advantages and disadvantages of living at home and compare them with the other types of accommodation.

IN PAIRS

1 If you decided to move out and look for a place of your own, how would you set about finding it? Make a list of where you could find information about the sort of accommodation available for young people in your area. Find out how much it would cost in your area to rent: a) a single room; b) a flat. Would it cost more/less/about the same to rent a flat in Glasgow, London, Birmingham or Manchester?
2 Once you find a place to live in the area you want, at the price you can afford, there are lots of problems you'll have to face, and many responsibilities you'll have to take on. Discuss the problems you'll have to tackle and the new responsibilities you'll have. Make a list of extra expenses that you'll have to budget for when you live on your own, which you don't have to pay for when you live at home. (The article on page 18 will help you.)

Young and homeless

Many young people leave home and manage to set up on their own without too many problems. But a growing number of young people have difficulty finding anywhere to live, and end up homeless. Ted describes what it feels like to be constantly on the move between temporary accommodation, hostels and bed and breakfasts.

'I'm sure I don't need to tell many people how confidence-shattering and soul-destroying it is to be trapped in that position, with your few possessions scattered in various people's cellars and spare cupboards across a city. If you're lucky enough to have friends who can put you up for a while, you may risk losing their friendship. It's a downward spiral. I know people who have been homeless for four or five years, and that's in relatively easy places to find accommodation, such as Bath or Leicester.

When I went down to the council in Swindon to try and get on to their housing list – average waiting time for a single person, three years, incidentally – I was told that I couldn't be considered until I was actually living somewhere, so that they could assess my current conditions! I couldn't even fill in the form to get onto the list.'

IN PAIRS

1 What do you learn from Ted's story about the difficulties you may face as a homeless person?
2 If you become homeless, friends or relatives may put you up for a while. Discuss the difficulties that might arise in such a situation:
   How long do you think you might be able to stay?
   What would you do with all your belongings?
   What sort of conflicts might occur?
3 How many weeks or months would you or your family be willing to have a homeless friend or relative to stay?

FOR YOUR FOLDER

You work for a teenage magazine writing an advice column. Write an article entitled 'So you want to leave home?'. Advise your readers what they must think about and plan for – in particular, what it will cost – when deciding whether or not to leave home.

YOUR RIGHTS AS A CONSUMER

Asking for a refund

If your new tape recorder chews up your tapes, it is clearly a bad product. You should take it back to the shop and ask for your money back. Your rights to a refund for faulty goods are set out in the Sale of Goods Act 1979. This says you can return goods and get a refund in three cases:

1 If the goods are not of 'merchantable quality' (should not be sold in their condition).
2 If they are not 'fit for the purpose' (like chewing up tapes).
3 If they are not 'as described' (a jumper labelled 100% wool, but half acrylic).

You may not find it easy or pleasant to ask for a refund, but it's worth standing up for your rights.
Remember, you should go back to the shop where you bought the goods.

Five steps to a refund
If you are refused at one step, go to the next.

Step 1: Take the faulty item back to the shop. Tell them you want a refund and mention the Sale of Goods Act 1979.

Step 2: Ask to speak to the shop manager and repeat Step 1.

Step 3: Write to the shop and send a copy to their head office. Quote the Sale of Goods Act. Keep copies of the letters you and they write.

Step 4: Write directly to the head office and say you'll go to the small claims court (for goods under £500) or take legal advice if you don't get a refund within, say 10 days from the date of your letter.

Step 5: Take your claim to the small claims court. The Citizens Advice Bureau will advise you on this.

No matter what they say . . .
1 You don't need a receipt. Proof of purchase can be something like the shop's label or price tag.
2 You don't have to take a credit note, replacement or repair. You have a right to a refund if that's what you wish.
3 You don't have to allow the shop to send the goods back to the manufacturer for them to agree that they're faulty.
4 Pay no attention to signs saying 'No refunds'. These are illegal. But remember, you can't demand a refund if you just change your mind.

Secondhand goods

If you buy goods from a trader you have the same kind of rights under the Sale of Goods Act for secondhand goods as you do for new. However, you must take into account the age of the article, the price you are asked to pay and the description given by the trader.

If you buy from someone who is not a trader, then it is known as a private sale. You have fewer rights in this case, because the Sale of Goods Act says that goods sold privately only have to match their description.

IN GROUPS ══ *What are their rights?* ══

Discuss each of these cases. What are the person's rights? What do you think each of them should do?

JAYNE: I bought a purse at the market from a stall selling leather goods, but when I got home, I found it was plastic. Will I get a refund if I take it back.

LES: I bought a new video recorder but can't get it to work properly. When I went back to the shop, they said I'd have to contact the manufacturer because there wasn't anything they could do. Do I have to do this?

SUE: I bought this necklace in a sale. The first time I went to put it on, next day, the clasp broke. When I took it back, they refused to give me a refund.

TIM: I got a guarantee with my new bedside clock. The alarm won't work properly. Do I have to claim under the guarantee or can I get the shop to sort it out?

JAY: I bought this torch from a mate, but it won't work. Am I legally entitled to demand my money back?

LISA: I saw this secondhand bike advertised in the paper and went along and bought it. When I got home, I found one of the wheels was buckled. Is there anything I can do?

STEVE: I took my denim jacket into a cleaner's advertising a same day service. When I went to collect it, they said it wouldn't be ready for another two days. So when it was finally ready, I refused to pay and they refused to give it me back. What should I do now?

IN PAIRS ════

Role play a scene in which somebody takes back a new sports bag whose handle broke on the first use, the day after it was bought. Do the scene twice. First, show the person complaining in a loud, rude, aggressive way. Then repeat the scene showing them making their complaint politely but firmly.

▓ FOR YOUR FOLDER ▓

Imagine that you bought a new tape-recorder from a shop called Cheapo-Lines, 55 High Street, Oldtown OL5 3LT. Although it plays tapes all right, it distorts the sound whenever you try to make a recording. Write a letter of complaint asking the shop to give you a refund. You do not wish for a replacement or repair.

BUY NOW, PAY LATER

BUYING ON CREDIT

What is credit?

Credit is a way of borrowing money in order to buy goods or services now, and pay for them later.

How much do you have to pay for credit?

It depends on the type of credit. You'll normally have to pay a charge made up of interest plus other costs like administration fees. Traders offering credit have to tell you what their rate of charge is. This is called the APR and is normally 20% to 30% of the amount you borrow. You can work out how good a deal you are getting by comparing one APR with another.

What are the main ways you can get credit?

Some of the ways you can get credit are:

BANK LOANS

There are several kinds of bank loan. Two of the most common are *overdraft* (if you have a current account); and *personal loans*. You have to pay interest on both these.

BUDGET ACCOUNT

Many shops offer this type of credit. You agree to pay the shop a certain amount each month, and the shop agrees to give you credit of up to 24 times that amount. So, if you pay £10 a month, you can buy up to £240 worth of goods. You are charged interest on the amount left during each month.

CREDIT CARDS

● *Bank credit cards* (Access, Barclaycard, for example) You can use this card in any place that accepts it to buy goods and services on credit, even in foreign countries. Each cardholder is given a personal credit limit.

You have to pay off a certain amount of what you owe each month. If you pay the whole debt in one month, you don't pay interest. Otherwise, you are charged interest on the amount that is still owed.

● *Shop card* You can only use this card in the main shop and branches of the company that issues it. Credit limits, interest rates and conditions of use vary from shop to shop.

● *Charge card* (American Express, Diners etc.) You can use this card in any place that accepts it. You pay an annual membership fee rather than interest, and have to pay off the full amount at the end of each month.

HIRE PURCHASE

Many shops will arrange this type of credit for you through a finance company. You pay a certain sum as a deposit. Then you pay the rest over a set period in regular amounts. HP can be an expensive way of borrowing, so it is worth looking closely at what the APR is before you sign an agreement.

CREDIT SALES

This is similar to hire purchase except that you immediately own the goods you buy.

FINANCE COMPANY PERSONAL LOAN

If you are buying a large item such as a motorbike or stereo system, the trader may arrange a loan for you through a finance company. You have to pay the loan back over a set time and are charged interest. Terms may vary from company to company.

MAIL ORDER CATALOGUES

You select the goods you want from the catalogue and pay for them over a period of time, normally not more than 20 weeks. You do not pay any interest.

MONEYLENDERS

Moneylenders often give loans when no one else will. They will arrange many types of loans, but interest rates can be very high. Be careful that the moneylender is licensed if you ever have to go to one.

Before you buy on credit . . .

Ask yourself these questions:

● **What would the item cost if I paid cash?**
● **What is the difference between the credit price and the cash price?**
● **Can I afford the repayments?**
● **Do I really need the item now? Can't I wait to get it?**
● **How long would it take me to save the money to buy it for cash?**
● **What is the amount I would pay in interest?**
● **If I wait and save up to buy it, what could I buy with the extra money that would otherwise have gone in interest payments?**

IN PAIRS

Sue earns £15 a week from her Saturday job and baby-sitting. She has put by £50 since she started to save. She reckons she can save at the rate of £7.50 a week. She wants to buy herself a good stereo system. Should she buy it now on credit, or wait until she has saved up the full price? What is your advice?

IN GROUPS

What are the main advantages and disadvantages of buying goods on credit? Discuss the various ways of obtaining credit. What are the good points and drawbacks of each one? If you wanted credit, which method or methods would you choose?

Which method or methods would you never use?

What does it cost?

Interest rates differ from one credit card to another. The usual amount is around 2.5% per month but, like everything else, it can go up – sometimes sharply. You are, after all, borrowing money. If you buy a sweater for £20 and pay £1 when you are billed, you will have to pay £1 plus the interest rate the following month. If you continue to pay only the £1 a month, that £20 sweater could cost you over £30 in the end. So beware. Interest has a nasty habit of taking you unawares. If you pay your bill in full each month, though, you won't be charged a penny extra.

PROS...

- Specific shop cards can be very useful if you shop in one place regularly.
- Credit or option cards cut down on the amount of cash that you have to carry around.
- You can buy something instantly and pay later, which is great if you have pay, pocket money or a grant coming in regularly.
- You can afford to buy things that are just that little bit out of your reach.
- You can use most cards all over the country and, in some cases, overseas.

CONS...

- Used carelessly, these cards can be lethal. You can spend so much that you stay in debt for months or years.
- Interest rates are very high. If you don't pay all you owe at the end of the month, you pay a good bit extra the following month.
- Credit cards encourage you to spend more than you can afford.
- You can be lured into buying things you don't need just because your card is to hand.
- Not everyone can cope with a credit card, and you might be one of these people. For you, they're not worth the hassle and the worry.

Only themselves to blame?

by ANNE BARROWCLOUGH

LOUISE, a 23-year-old secretary, takes home £130 a week. But she is penniless . . . Because of a spending spree last Christmas – done entirely on credit – she is now £3,000 in debt to eight different credit companies. It took her less than three months to run up the debt. It will take her at least two years to clear it.

Louise is one of thousands of young victims of the credit boom. Like so many other young people, she was lured into overspending by the ease of borrowing and the proliferation of credit cards.

Over the past year, the largest group of debtors has been pinpointed as the 18-25 age group.

Many are school-leavers in their first job who falsely believe that their first income will cover their debts. Others are university students who find themselves unable to budget on their university grants.

Louise's story is becoming increasingly common among her generation. And the amount she owes is a great deal less than many others.

IN GROUPS

Discuss these questions, then report your views to the rest of the class. What do you learn about the dangers of using credit cards from the newspaper article? Do you think the advantages of having credit cards outweigh the disadvantages? You cannot usually get a credit card until you are 18. Do you think the age restriction is right? Should it be lowered to 16? Raised to 21? Should there be other restrictions.

Draw up a set of rules giving advice to young people: Do's and Don'ts – How to use your credit cards wisely.

ROLE PLAY IN PAIRS

Ian has run up a huge debt on credit cards. He telephones you for advice. Role play the conversation in which you discuss what he should do.

FOR YOUR FOLDER

Work with a partner. Make up a story about a young person or a young couple who get into debt because they buy too much on credit.

WHER

CAREERS OFFICE

The careers office has details of local firms which have vacancies and are looking for school leavers to hire. It also has details of YTS schemes.

JOBCENTRE

Most jobs on the Jobcentre's self-selection stands are for adults. So if you see an interesting vacancy, check that it is suitable for a young person. Jobcentres can also give you information about government training courses and employment programmes.

LOCAL SERVICES

There are special services in certain towns, set up by local radio stations or the Manpower Services Commission. Contact any special services in your area and either send for information or join any schemes they run.

EMPLOYMENT AGENCY

Most employment agencies specialise in office jobs. Often the jobs are for people with training, such as word processor operators. But there is no harm in enquiring here. It won't cost you anything, because the agency charges the firm which does the hiring. Don't use an agency that asks *you* for a fee or part of your wages as commission for finding you a job.

VACANCY BOARD AND CARDS

Some firms, such as fast-food chains like Macdonalds, advertise vacancies on boards at the counter or in the window. Sometimes there are vacancy cards in news-agents' windows. But the majority of such adverts are for part-time jobs, mainly cleaning.

NEWSPAPER

Local newspapers carry job adverts in their 'situations vacant' columns. Since advertisements cost money, many of them are brief with many abbreviations. So it is often worth checking whether the job is suitable for a school leaver before you apply. Vacancies are often filled quickly. So if you see something that interests you, act immediately. **Trade Magazines** advertize jobs in particular fields such as farming or nursing. They often want someone trained but it may be worth checking.

PARENTS, RELATIVES AND FRIENDS

Many young people find a job through someone they know personally, either in the family or friends. It is worth letting many people know you want a job, so they can let you know if something suitable comes up.

APPLYING FOR A JOB BY PHONE

When you're looking at advertisements for jobs, you'll find that a lot of them ask you to phone for further details. You needn't get nervous about this if you get yourself organised before you start.

1 READ THE ADVERTISEMENT

First, read the advertisement carefully to make sure the job is suitable for you. There's no point in applying for a job in a warehouse if you know that you'd collapse after lifting up a five-pound weight.

2 MAKE NOTES BEFORE YOU PHONE

When you phone, the employer will probably ask you some questions about yourself. It can be quite hard to remember even simple facts, like the dates you have been at school. So write out the main points from your CV (see page 30).

3 KNOW WHY YOU ARE SUITABLE

Think about why you want the job, or why you think you'd be good at it. The employer is very likely to ask you this. It's a good idea to look at your interests and activites as well as your school work and see if they help.

4 ASK QUESTIONS

Think about what you need to know. What questions do you want to ask? For example, "What exactly does the job involve?" "Would I receive any training?" "What are the hours of work?" "Is there any weekend work or evening work?"

5 PLAN AHEAD

The employer may well ask you to come along and have a chat, or there may be formal interview times. So make sure you know when you're free.

'O LOOK

IN PAIRS

Many people waste a lot of time applying for jobs which are not right for them. The chart on the right is designed to help you get the information you need from job advertisements. Study a number of newspaper adverts and fill in an information check chart like this for each one.

Note: Newspaper adverts often do not include all this information. If any item on your check chart is missing, it is worth phoning to get the information before making an application.

Your school's visiting Careers Officer can advise you about jobs.

Information check chart

Name of newspaper ....

Date of issue ....

Name of firm advertising ....

Job title ....

Location of job ....

Person to contact ....

Address of firm ....

Telephone number to ring ....

Starting date ....

Age restrictions (if any) ....

Qualifications required ....
(if any)

Starting pay ....

Training and prospects
(if any)

6 PRACTISE THE PHONECALL

When you've got all this information together, you've done most of the preparation. But telephoning about jobs is rather different from ringing your friends – and it's as well to have some practice conversations with a friend. Once you've done this, you're ready to phone for the real job.

7 MAKING THE PHONECALL

When you're phoning, bear the following points in mind.

▶ **MAKE SURE YOU HAVE** the advertisement, your personal details, questions you want to ask the employer, paper and pen to take down information.

▶ **IF YOU HAVE TO USE A PUBLIC CALL BOX** make sure it's in a quiet area – not in a railway station or near a juke box, for example. It's worth finding one of the newer public phones where there are no pips to interrupt the call. Make sure you have plenty of coins with you – you don't want to get cut off in the middle of the call. If you can, buy a phone card.

▶ **PHONE AT A SENSIBLE TIME:** Check the advertisement to see if it gives times for phoning. If

not, phone during normal working hours, but avoid lunchtime. It might be the most convenient time for you, but the employer is quite likely to be out.

▶ **TALK TO THE RIGHT PERSON:** When the phone is answered, first ask to speak to the person whose name is given in the advertisement. If there is no name given, just say which job you're ringing about and ask if you can speak to someone about it.

▶ **SAY WHO YOU ARE:** When you get through to the right person, give your name and say you're phoning about the job advertised in _____ (where you saw it). Ask if there is still a vacancy.

▶ **USE YOUR CV:** The employer will probably ask you a few questions. Have your CV notes to hand and use them to answer these.

▶ **TAKE NOTES:** If the employer asks you to come for an interview, write down the day and time you're expected and the name of the person you should ask to see. Also make sure you have the right address of the company and, if necessary, ask for and write down directions to get there.

▶ **SAY THANK YOU:** Thank the employer at the end of the conversation and check your appointment day and time.

ROLE PLAY

From your local paper, choose a job advert that asks for applications by phone. Role play the conversation between an applicant and the employer. Take it in turns to be the applicant. Before you begin, prepare for the role play by listing the questions the employer will ask.

FOR YOUR FOLDER

STOCKROOM and junior sales assistant required for happy West End chemist. 5 day week. suitable school leaver. — Mr Jeffrey. 723 8711. SH-76-7

Study the advert above. Then write the script of the telephone conversation between the employer and an applicant who is interested in the job. You do not have to make the applicant do everything right. You could write a script which shows the job seeker making all kinds of mistakes, because they have not prepared for the telephone call before making it.

Writing a letter of application

Each letter you write applying for a job can be much the same, except that you should highlight any experience that is relevant for the particular job. You should send a CV (see pages 30–31) with each letter of application.

Write your letter in blue or black ink or type. If you can use a word processor, this is a good time to do so. It will show that you can handle new technology. Perhaps your school will let you use their equipment for this important purpose. Each letter should be individually written or typed, not photocopied. Each letter should include the following points:

Addresses
Your full address, including postcode, in the top right hand corner. The employer's name and address, in full, slightly below your address and on the left hand side of the paper. Make sure you spell their name and address correctly.

Date and reference
The date and reference number in the advert, if any, in the top right hand corner under your address.

Beginning and ending the letter
If a name is given in the advertisement, address your letter to that person and begin 'Dear Ms Fraser'. End the letter 'Yours sincerely'. If there is no name, but only a title such as The Personnel Manager, then begin the letter 'Dear Sir or Madam' and end it 'Yours faithfully'. If the advertisement tells you only the company's name, such as 'Apply A&A Appliances', then address your letter to The Manager and begin it 'Dear Sir or Madam'.

First paragraph
Say the name of the job you are applying for and where you heard or read about the job.

Second paragraph
A little bit about yourself. Just your age and what you are doing now is sufficient. The details are in your CV.

Third paragraph
This is the part of the letter you will have to think about for each job. You should say why you want that particular job, or mention some experience that is relevant. If you can't think of anything else to write, try 'I would like to work in an office' or 'I am interested in learning about . . .' It is a positive statement and shows you are interested. Think about what the job involves and what experience you have had that is relevant.

Applying for jobs 'on spec'

Even if a firm you want to work for has not advertised a vacancy, try writing or phoning 'on spec'. At worst it will cost a few pence, and at best it could lead to a job.

Who to write to?
You could ring up the firm and ask the switchboard for the name of the person who deals with recruitment. Otherwise, address your letter to 'The Manager' or 'The Personnel Manager' and begin it 'Dear Sir or Madam'.

What to say?
Writing a letter 'on spec' is much the same as writing a letter answering an advert. Begin your letter positively:

Dear Sir or Madam,
        I am keen to make a career in engineering and am writing to ask if you have any vacancies for trainees now or in the near future.

Dear Ms Smith,
        I am looking forward to starting my first job. I would like to work in a shop and am writing to ask you if you have any vacancies for school leavers.

SUPAH SUPERMARKETS

Young person with good general education required to train as sales assistant. Must work all day Saturdays.

Write to Ms Hedsen
Supah Supermarkets
Tracey Street
Sheffield S8 4DB

Ref 2/84/AG

IN PAIRS

Read Martin Weller's letter to Ms Hedsen. The labels A – M show important points in his letter of application. Make a list from A – M saying what points Martin Weller is making, for example: A – your address.

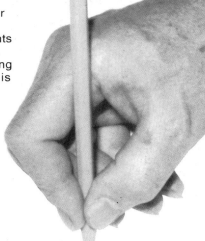

Martin Weller wrote this letter in reply:

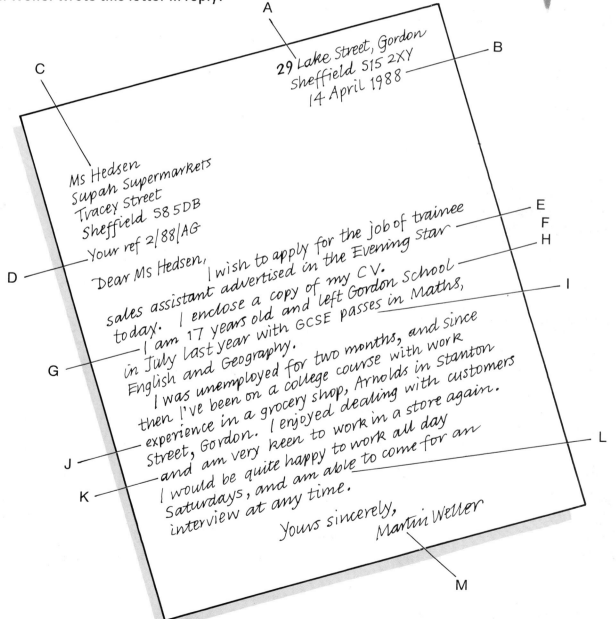

A — 29 Lake Street, Gordon
B — Sheffield S15 2XY
14 April 1988

C —
Ms Hedsen
Supah Supermarkets
Tracey Street
Sheffield S8 5DB
D — Your ref 2/88/AG

Dear Ms Hedsen,

E — I wish to apply for the job of trainee
F — sales assistant advertised in the Evening Star
H — today. I enclose a copy of my CV.
G — I am 17 years old and left Gordon School
I — in July last year with GCSE passes in Maths, English and Geography.

I was unemployed for two months, and since
then I've been on a college course with work
J — experience in a grocery shop, Arnolds in Stanton
Street, Gordon. I enjoyed dealing with customers
K — and am very keen to work in a store again.

I would be quite happy to work all day
Saturdays, and am able to come for an
L — interview at any time.

Yours sincerely,
Martin Weller
M —

The Curriculum Vitae (CV)

Your letter of application is not enough. You should include a curriculum vitae, which is commonly called a CV. This is a short account of a person's working career with personal details and information about qualifications, education and interests. It is important even though you do not have any work experience, because it gives the person who might employ you a quick picture of you, and it saves you putting everything in a letter every time you write one. Remember to include references on your CV. Normally you will want two. One of these should be your school head or a senior member of staff. The other can be a family friend who has known you for a long time, your doctor, the vicar, or the like.

IN PAIRS

Look at the illustration below and decide why the manager is frowning at the CV she is holding. List three improvements that the CV writer should make next time she applies for a job.

FOR YOUR FOLDER

Study Sandra Gregg's CV. Then draft a CV of your own. Before you copy it out, show your draft to a friend. Discuss it together and see if there is anything important you have left out. Don't be afraid to include all your good points and achievements. Remember you are trying to make a good impression on the person who might employ you.

Curriculum Vitae

NAME: Sandra Gregg

DATE OF BIRTH: 26.6.72

ADDRESS: 44 Greystoke Road
                         Anderbury
                         Nr Preston
                         Lancashire LA3 6PY

                         Telephone: (0246) 2034

EDUCATION: St George's Comprehensive School 1983-88
                         Preston Road
                         Anderbury
                         LA3 8NW

EXAMINATIONS: GCSE English
                              Maths
                              Art
                              Biology
                              Physics
                              Geography
                              Drama
                              Business Studies
                         Awaiting results

INTERESTS: Computers, dancing, drama
                         Member of Girls Venture Corps

OTHER INFORMATION: Took part in French Exchange 1986
                         Assisted with stage lighting at
                          various school productions
                         Duke of Edinburgh Gold Award
                         Part-time work as shop assistant
                          in North's Bakery Summer 1987
                         One week work experience in the
                          clerical department at Moors
                         Components November 1987

REFEREES: Ms G Bledlow
                         Head Teacher
                         St George's School
                         Anderbury

                         Mr R Barne
                         15 Grove Road
                         Anderbury
                         (Family friend)

INTERVIEWS

Before the interview

JOB INTERVIEW CHECKLIST

Alastair Evans of the Institute of Personnel Management offers a checklist for going to a job interview.

1 Before the interview read any letters or leaflets sent to you by the prospective employers – and make sure you have done everything they ask you to do.

2 Find out as much as you can about the organisation from your parents, friends, teachers or local library.

3 Make a list in advance of questions you might want to ask the interviewers about the job itself, pay and conditions, and the organisation.

4 Think in advance about the questions the interviewers are likely to ask you – about your school career, special achievements, sports, hobbies, or responsibilities you have taken on – and plan the answers you will give.

5 Sort out the journey you have to make beforehand, find out how long it takes – and make sure you arrive with time to spare.

6 Dress smartly, be neat and tidy in appearance and well-groomed.

7 Aim to tell the interviewers as much as you can about yourself and why you think you could do the job.

8 Before going to the interview work out in your own mind what your strengths and abilities are – and be sure you try to get them across.

At the interview

● Try not to be nervous. Be polite and friendly.

● Concentrate on the questions asked. Take time to think before answering, but not too long.

● Don't worry about other things like the employer taking notes or papers on the desk.

● Try to answer the questions fully in a straight-forward and sure way. Try to look at the employer rather than round the room.

● If you have done similar work before, say so. If not, say you are keen to try.

● Show that you're interested in the job and ask questions about the duties, conditions and prospects.

● Don't criticise previous employers.

● Don't smoke unless invited to do so.

IN PAIRS

Put yourself in the interviewer's place. What would you look for in people applying for a job? Select one of these jobs: hotel receptionist, chef, garage mechanic, sales assistant in department store, laboratory technician, accounts clerk, hairdresser, police officer.

1 Each copy out the list below. Put a tick beside the things you think are important for the job your pair selected, and a cross beside the ones you think unimportant.

Neatly dressed	Relaxed manner
Bright and alert	Hair neat and tidy
Shy	Matching clothes
Serious manner	Non-smoker
Laughs easily	Good looking
Not overweight	Wearing expensive looking jewellery
Punctual	Looks fit and strong

2 Work out a list of questions that the employer might ask you at the interview.

3 Work out another list of questions the job seeker should ask at the interview.

ROLE PLAY

One of you play the interviewer and one the job applicant. Then take it in turns to show your role plays to the rest of your class. Discuss each job seeker's performance.

UNEMPLOYMENT

What to do if you don't get a job

If you're under 18, go to your careers office and register for work.

' If you're 18 or over, sign on at your nearest Unemployment Benefit office. Then start looking for work at any Jobcentre. You don't have to register there, but you may find it helpful. You're also free to use the careers office if you wish.

Unemployment Benefit

If you've just left school you probably won't be able to get Unemployment Benefit because it's a National Insurance benefit, and you probably won't have paid enough – or any – Class 1 NI contributions. If in doubt, ask at the Unemployment Benefit office. To get Unemployment Benefit, you must also be actively looking for a job and able and available to take up any suitable full-time work (including approved training schemes, such as the Youth training Scheme (YTS)).

How much? Unemployment Benefit is £32.75 a week (April 1988 rates).

How to claim If you're under 18 and think you may be entitled to Unemployment Benefit, take your P45 form (if you've got one) and your NI Numbercard to your careers office. They will give you a card to take to the Unemployment Benefit office. (You will only have a P45 form if you've worked for an employer. It is the form your employer gives you when you leave and shows how much tax you've paid.)

If you're 18 or over take your P45 and NI Numbercard to the Unemployment Benefit office. Go on the first day you're unemployed or you may lose some benefit.

If you lose your job

If you lose your job and you're under 18, go to your careers office and register for work. Tell them if you also intend to sign on at the Unemployment Benefit office.

If you're 18 or over, sign on immediately at your nearest Unemployment Benefit office. You can then start looking for another job at any Jobcentre. You don't have to register there, but you may find it helpful. You're also free to use the careers office if you wish.

Income Support – help if you're on a low income

If you haven't got a job and don't have enough money to live on, you may be able to get *Income Support*. The rules about 16 and 17 year olds claiming income support changed in September 1988. Most young people of this age can no longer claim income support. But you may be able to claim income support if you are bringing up a child on your own or if you are disabled and unlikely to be able to get a job.

How to claim If you're under 18, go to the careers office. They will give you a card to take to the Unemployment Benefit office.

If you're 18 or over, go to the Un-

employment Benefit office, claim Unemployment Benefit and ask for an Income Support claim form. Fill it in and send it to your Social Security office. You will be given an addressed postage-paid envelope.

The Social Security office will arrange for your Income Support to be paid to you by the Unemployment Benefit office.

More information *For more information* about Income Support see leaflet SB 1 *Income Support – Cash help* or leaflet SB 20 *A guide to Income Support.*

Voluntary unemployment

If you're unemployed because:
  you've left your job or an approved training scheme (such as YTS) without good reason,
or you've been dismissed from your job or an approved training scheme for misconduct,
or you've refused, without good reason, to apply for or accept a suitable job or place on an approved training scheme,
or you've failed, without good reason, to follow official advice to help you find a suitable job or training place,

you may be regarded as voluntarily unemployed. If so, either or both of the following will apply:
● you may not be paid Unemployment Benefit for up to 26 weeks.
● if you're getting Income Support, it will be reduced for up to 26 weeks.

ELENI SAUNDERS

Eleni didn't discover she could sign on until a year after leaving school. She spent the next five years getting more and more fed up. **'The worst thing is never having any money, and wondering if you're going to spend the rest of your life like this.'** Then Eleni got involved with a project for young unemployed women. **'It helped me to see possibilities and gave me a clear idea of what I wanted to do.'**

She is now employed by the Youth Unemployment Resource Centre and is hoping to get on to a Youth Work training course.

PETER SAMUELS

Peter Samuels left school and went straight into a job paint spraying cars. Two-and-a-half years later the firm went bust. Since then Peter has been in and out of jobs and has now been unemployed for a year-and-a-half.

'I want to work', he says, **'but I can't find anything I like as much as spray painting'.** His benefit pays for the rent on a flat in north-east London. **'The worst thing is the amount of time you've got to kill'**, he says. So he's looking for a local youth club to join to pass the time.

GINA'S PROBLEM

I've just left school and I haven't got a job yet, though I've had a couple of interviews. I'm worried about what I'm going to do for money until I find one. My friend says I can't claim the dole because I'm not old enough. My mum says she'll throw me out if I don't start paying something towards my keep. Is there anything I can do?

Gina

FOR YOUR FOLDER

Study the information given on this page and write a reply to Gina.

COPING WITH *REJECTION*

In any one day, we may all face scores of rejections from slight to great. We may be ignored at the prescription counter at the chemist's, or overlooked for promotion, or turned down for a job we really want.

We all feel rejected at some time or other. We have to learn to cope with it. How well we cope with rejection affects how we appear to others and also how we feel about ourselves.

"I can't describe how bad it was. It just consumed me and it was all I could think about. We were both at the same college and, when the holidays came, my girlfriend went away to France for a month. When she came back, she had changed so much and it was obvious that the relationship was going to end. To cap it all, the day she came back was my birthday and we went out for the most awful meal. At the end of the evening, she just said: 'Look, I've changed. I don't think we can see each other any more.' Then we went back to college and, although I saw her every day, we didn't speak to each other at all.

"I had a constant sort of wrenching, tight feeling in my stomach and it was as though I didn't want to live in my body. I felt so desperate and tense all the time. The only way to relieve the tension was to cry. I couldn't read or listen to records, because I was literally too sad. She haunted me to the point where I could feel myself just falling apart. Then, to make it worse, a post-card from France arrived – it had been delayed in a postal strike – telling me that she was missing me and really looking forward to seeing me. I just broke down."

Daniel, 19

"When I was at school, I had a really good friend – Cheryl. We went everywhere together. I never thought we'd stop being friends, even when I went away to college and she moved in with her boyfriend, Ian.

"I *did* worry that we'd have less in common but that never seemed to happen.

"And then suddenly one day, she didn't want to know me any more. She didn't say it in so many words but she came up with really feeble excuses: Ian's parents were coming for tea; she was too tired; she'd call and arrange something – but she never did.

"I finally rang her up and said I was a bit upset that she was making so little effort to see me. She didn't deny it. She just said (and I can remember her tone of voice to this day) 'I'm sorry you feel like that. See you around'.

"I haven't seen her since. For a while, I was really depressed. What had I said? What had I done? I was convinced it was *my* fault.

"Being given the elbow does that to you. Now I realise that we no longer had anything in common. I'm still sad that I've lost a bit of my past by losing a friend, and that hurts. But she has too, and she'll be regretting it long after I've got over it."

Suzanne, 20

"I've been unemployed for almost nine months now and it's really getting me down.

"I mean, how can you keep writing off for jobs (and sometimes going for interviews) when you know you're more than likely going to be rejected?

"The last job I went for was a sales assistant in a big record store. I'm good with figures. I like talking to people and all my friends can vouch for the fact that I'm a walking encyclopaedia of pop. So I was sure I'd be in with a chance. But, of course, I didn't get the job and that really got me down.

"The thing is, you can't help thinking that there's something wrong with *you*. If 50 people apply and then 10 are put on the short-list because they have the right qualifications, the final decision has to be made on personality, right? And when you keep being turned down for jobs, you begin to think you don't have the right personality.

"Yes, I know my other friends have the same problems as me. After all, there are almost four million unemployed. But that doesn't make me feel any better. That doesn't stop me feeling any less useless.

"I've got a feeling that I've got a neon sign coming out of my head which says: 'This girl is useless'. It's a bit like dogs attacking you because they know you're frightened of them. I feel useless so I come over useless, therefore nobody wants to give me a job . . ."

Claudette, 17

Think the following thoughts and you'll never get out of the rejection trap. Be aware of them and you'll soon see a big change in your feelings.

● **One failure means I'll always fail.**
Of course is doesn't. Learn to think of each situation separately, not as part of an changeable pattern. Everyone fails sometimes.

● **I know he's going to go off me.**
How can you be so sure people are going to act the way you think they will? Let things take their course naturally.

● **They said they thought I'd be right for the job but they were probably only being kind.**
Think positive. If they said it, they might just have meant it.

● **It's my fault we broke up.**
Don't blame yourself for everything. You're only 50 per cent of a relationship, so you can't be 100 per cent to blame.

● **She said I was thick so I must be.**
Thinking badly of yourself won't help. Think about when it was said, how it was said and who said it.

● **But he turned me down.**
No is just no, not the end of the world.

● **What will people think?**
What you think is what matters. Perhaps this is one of the hardest lessons

A It was my birthday last week and I only got six cards. But when my friend had her birthday, she must have got over 20. She's got so many more friends and relations than I have! At birthdays and Christmas she always gets more cards and presents than I do. It makes me feel there must be something wrong with me because she's so popular and I'm not. What can I do to make people like me more?

B It was the first interview I've had. But I knew the moment I got there I'd never get the job. All the other job applicants were older than I am and had more qualifications. I didn't stand a chance. It made me feel so useless. It's just not worth bothering to apply for any more jobs!

C I spent ages choosing her present. But when I gave it to her, she didn't seem particularly pleased. She was far more interested in the sound system her mum and dad gave her. If I try to say anything, she'll just tell me not to be so childish. What should I do? It's really got me down.

D When I got accepted on the course at college, I went straight round to tell my friend. But he didn't seem very interested. Since then he's been very offhand, and every time I ring up to suggest doing something together, he just makes an excuse and rings off. What have I done wrong?

E I went out with this girl and I thought we got on really well together. We had a great laugh. Then,

FEELING REJECTED

when I asked her if she'd see me again, she just said 'no'. When I asked her why not, she just said she didn't want to. It made me feel so miserable, because I really fancied her.

F Everyone's talking about this party they are all going to. But I haven't been invited. I'm sure it's out of spite, and that the person who is giving the party wants to get at me. I feel so left out.

G I spent ages on my art project and my teacher said it's the best thing I've done. But when I took it home to show Mum, she hardly glanced at it and just got on with the work she was doing. Yet if my baby brother brings something home from playgroup, she always makes a fuss over it. It's not fair. What can I do to get her interested in the things I do?

H My friend needs some money so that she can go on the school trip abroad with the rest of us. I've got plenty just now because I've recently had my birthday. But when I offered to lend her some, she just snapped at me. Why won't she accept my offer? I feel so hurt.

I A couple of months ago, my best friend told me she didn't want to be my best friend any more. I was really hurt. We've been so close for four years. I still really like her, but everyone said I let her have her own way too much and let her push me around. My parents and friends tell me to forget her, but I can't.

to learn, but it's certainly one of the most important.

Once you've got used to the idea that not everything in life will come your way, and that it isn't necessarily your fault, you're likely to find that rejection isn't as tough to come to terms with as you thought.

We all survive rejection and it can even make us stronger in the long run.

After all, unless you try for something, you'll never know how successful you might have been . . .

IN GROUPS

Work in a group of six. Divide yourselves into three pairs. Each pair choose three of the situations, above, in which a person describes their feeling of rejection. What advice would you give in each case? Write down your advice. Then, in your group, discuss each situation in turn and say whether or not you agree with the advice.

FOR YOUR FOLDER

Think of a situation in which you have felt rejected. Which sort of rejection did you feel: unwanted? ignored? useless? unimportant? left out? a failure? hurt? resentful? Note down what you felt and what you actually did or said at the time. Did you express your feelings or not? Looking back, how well do you think you coped with the rejection? Do you wish you had handled things differently? If so, how? How would you cope with a similar situation in the future? Write about what happened, saying what your feelings were at the time and what your feelings are about it now.

Coping with grief

The feeling of loss that hits you when someone close to you dies is the strongest of human emotions. Grief often develops in quite definite stages. The first reaction is one of shock and numbness. Next, there is a feeling of deep distress that is so strong it is almost like a physical pain. Then may come sorrow and depression, anger, bitterness, guilt. Often these emotions are mixed. Finally, the bereaved person begins to let go, starting to accept the death and allowing fond memories to replace the pain. These stages often overlap and the period of mourning can take from a few months to many years.

Below are extracts from the book *Letters to Judy* compiled by the American author Judy Blume. She receives nearly 2,000 letters a month from young people.

The death of a parent

Dear Judy,
Hi! My name is Simone. I'm 14. In September I will go to high school. But I feel scared. I don't know how to tell you my feelings. My dad died last year soon after we came to America. He got cancer. I got so sad. Still, I didn't tell my friends that he died. I just didn't want to. But sometimes they ask about my parents like, "Are your parents split?" or questions like that. I don't know what to tell them.

Simone, age 14

I know how hard it is to lose someone you love. My father died suddenly, when I was 21.

I couldn't talk about my father's death to my mother. It's been 25 years and I still can't. But I was able to talk to other people and even now I can reminisce about him with some of my old friends. No matter what your age it's important to be able to talk about your feelings and about the person you love who has died. Talking about it helps you accept it and it helps to keep memories alive.

The death of a relative

Dear Judy,
My grandmother died two years ago. She had a stroke. For a few months I felt numb and I didn't cry. Then one night I was talking to a friend about grandparents and I just started to cry. After I did I felt a lot better. Now I can talk about my grandmother and I don't feel sad. I feel the love I have for her.

Susan, age 11

My grandmother (my mother's mother) was sick for a long time before she died from cancer. We had been very close. She lived with us for the two school years we spent in Florida and even after our return to New Jersey, she spent a lot of time at our house, although she made her home with my aunt and uncle. Because they both worked, she moved in with us when she became ill, so my mother could care for her.

No one really talked to me about her illness. I was a young teenager and I knew it was serious . . . My grandmother went to hospital for the last time a few weeks before I went away to summer camp. I visited her the day before I left but I didn't really know what to say or how to act. My mother said that Nanny was happy just to see me.

My parents called me at camp a month later, to tell me that my grandmother had died. The call came during dinner. When I heard the news I couldn't speak, I couldn't respond at all. I felt this gigantic lump in my throat and I hung up the phone before my parents were finished talking to me. They called right back to see if I was all right. I managed to say that I was. Then I returned to the dining hall and took my place at the table. But I couldn't eat. Rachel, my friend from home, asked me what was wrong. I whispered that my grandmother had died. Then I stood up and ran out of the dining hall. Rachel followed me. Although we hadn't been close that summer she knew my grandmother and she understood what I was feeling.

I didn't attend the evening activity. I sat outside under a tree, by myself, looking at the stars. After a while a counselor came and sat with me. He talked to me about death, about losing someone you love. He encouraged me to talk to him. But I wasn't ready to talk about my grandmother or to share what I was feeling.

I didn't go home for my grandmother's funeral. My parents thought it would be better for me to stay at camp . . . They were trying to protect me.

Now I believe it would have been better if I had gone to her funeral. I was 15 and my grandmother had been an important part of my life. I should have been there to say goodbye, and to share the sorrow of my family.

- Be careful not to avoid the person. Make a point of seeing them and saying 'I'm sorry'. If you find this hard to do, send a card or letter first. Bereaved people say that cards and letters of condolence are a great comfort.

- Give the bereaved person the opportunity to talk, and let them cry. Take your cue from them, but try not to join them in making judgements like 'Yes, the doctor didn't do enough.'

- Try to understand that guilt is often part of grief. For example, a bereaved parent might say: 'If only I hadn't let him have such a powerful motorbike.'

- If you feel overwhelmed by the strength of the person's emotions, then back off a little. Remember you are not the cause of the grief. You are simply helping them by letting them express their feelings.

- Offer to do some practical tasks like the shopping, housework, baby-sitting.

How you can help someone who has been bereaved

- Don't worry if the person is full of self-pity. This emotion is an important part of the healing process.

- If the bereaved person goes away for a while, contact them when they return.

- Try to encourage them to take reasonable care of themselves, such as eating enough and getting enough sleep. Don't stop inviting them to take part in things, but don't pressurise them to join in if they refuse your invitations.

- People who have been bereaved feel particularly low at Christmas and other joyous holidays, and on the birthday and anniversary of the day of death of their loved one. Encourage them to write down thoughts and feelings at such times, or send them a special bouquet of flowers. These actions often help them.

- If they cannot seem to cope, encourage them to contact a professional counselling service such as a youth counselling service, Cruse (for widows and widowers), the Samaritans (with phone service at any hour of the day or night). You can leave names and phone numbers of suitable organisations by the phone as a gentle hint, and to make it easy for them to ring.

IN GROUPS

1 The death of someone we love is something we all have to face sooner or later, yet most people are still embarrassed about expressing their private sorrow in public. For example, at one funeral a mother stopped her teenage daughter from crying over her father's grave with the words 'Come on! We've got this far without breaking down. Don't start now.'

Why are people in Britain embarrassed or ashamed to show their grief in public? What do you think of the widow's attitude towards her daughter's crying? Should you attempt to keep a stiff upper lip and control your emotions in public? Is it all right for women to show their grief, but not for men?

Choose a person to take notes. Discuss these questions and then have a spokesperson report your views to the rest of the class, using the notes that were made.

2 Mourning customs differ from one culture to another. Among cultures in which mourning is a ritual, health and emotional problems from grief are rare. In Britain, on the other hand, about one third of people who lose a wife or husband develop health or emotional problems of some kind.

Each choose a different culture and find out about its funeral and mourning customs. Then share the information in a group discussion.

IN PAIRS

Discuss these questions in pairs, then form groups and compare your views.
1 Judy Blume says she did not go to her grandmother's funeral. Were her parents right to stop her from going? Give your reasons.
2 Should children be allowed to attend only the funerals of immediate family – their parents or brothers and sisters – until they reach a certain age? Should they be protected from this emotional experience even for their immediate family?
3 If a relative or friend is dying, should a child be told? Is there an age, say, 7, 10, 12 or 14, after which children should be told? Or should they be told whatever age they are? Do you think it makes it easier for a child if they are forewarned of a person's death?

CLASS DISCUSSION

Why do people find it hard to talk to a bereaved person? Is it because nowadays death is something that normally happens in hospital rather than at home, so we are unfamiliar with it and frightened by it? Is it because death is regarded by many people as a taboo subject, so no one talks about it except when it actually happens?

FOR YOUR FOLDER

A letter of condolence to give sympathy to a bereaved person is not easy to write. Imagine your great uncle has died. You did not know him very well because he was housebound, but you have met your great aunt several times. They always send you a present for your birthday and Christmas. Draft a letter of condolence to your great-aunt, then show it to the others in the group. Read each other's and decide who has done the best job of expressing sympathy. Then, redraft your own letter and put the final version in your folder.

YOUR POLITICAL VIEWS

We need a pay rise

TAXES ARE TOO HIGH!

Theres too Much Crime

THE ROADS ARE TOO BUSY

BAN THE BOMB

we need more nursery schools

'What's it got to do with me?'

'*Ever since I was little, I've chosen friends from people I could talk to, so anyone who is racist, sexist or whatever, I couldn't get on with them. I have non-political friends in the sense of people who can't decide which party to vote for. But politics is exactly how you live your life, so in that sense, all my friends are politically aware.*

I can fully understand when people don't vote. I'm sad, because every vote counts, but I can understand that you feel totally alienated from politics. If you look at the House of Commons, they all look alike, whatever bench they're sitting on. They're all white, middle aged, middle class men. The House of Commons is supposed to be representative of the people and it's very far from that.'

Vijay Naidu, aged 19

'*A lot of young people aren't very active because they're basically very sceptical. They think that politics is something that happens up there in Westminster and they can't possibly have an effect on it. I think it's absolutely our responsibility to make the Government do what we want them to do. It's our future.*

Young people should get up and stop pretending it's nothing to do with them. You're more important because you're young, because you're the people who are going to vote soon, have the jobs or the money or the right to choose whether you want the system we have now.'

Sarah Young, aged 17

IN PAIRS

Many aspects of our lives are controlled by laws. So, we are all affected by politics whether or not we get actively involved. In pairs make a list of some of the ways in which laws made by the government control our daily life.

IN GROUPS

Join up with another pair and compare your lists.

Discuss Sarah Young's and Vijay Naidu's views. How important do think it is for young people to take an active interest in politics? Discuss Vijay's views about the House of Commons.

DECIDING YOUR PRIORITIES

What·are·you worried·about?

YOUNG PEOPLE in Britain are concerned most about getting a job, about nuclear war and weapons and about famine and world poverty. But around a quarter of those interviewed in the first Young Guardian Carrick James Youth Survey said nothing much concerned them at all.

These are the main findings from a national sample of 10-17 year-old young people asked two main questions: Which of the problems facing this country today worries you most? Which of the problems facing the whole world worries you most? Those polled were also asked what other problems they thought important.

Of national problems, unemployment is the most widely felt, followed closely by nuclear weapons and war. Third are crime and violence. These were the only widespread concerns although many other problems were mentioned.

Age was a major influence on what worried youngsters. First, it affected whether any problem at all was mentioned. One in four of those questioned did not mention any problem. This group included 40 per cent of 10-11 year-olds, but only 15 per cent of the 16-17 year-olds.

There was a dramatic rise in concern about unemployment as a major problem, both as respondents got older (only one in ten of 10-11 year-olds, but nearly half 16-17 year-olds mentioned it); and as the poll moved north.

Worries about nuclear questions also increased with age while younger people were more bothered about violence and crime (including child abuse, kidnap and murder).

A broadly similar picture emerged for world problems, although famine and poverty topped the list in place of unemployment, both as the main and the most mentioned problem. Nuclear war and weapons again figured prominently, although as a world problem more boys than girls thought it important (34 per cent against 25 per cent).

Young people are also worried by issues as diverse as the Channel Tunnel and the spread of rabies, glue sniffing, litter, overpopulation and acid rain.

PRIORITIES & POLICIES

ON YOUR OWN

Write down your answers to the questions which young people were asked in the survey reported in the newspaper article on the left.

1 Which of the problems facing the country worries you most? Which other problems facing Britain are you worried about?

2 Which of the problems facing the whole world worries you most? Which other world problems are you worried about?

IN GROUPS

Discuss your answers then draw up lists of a) national issues; b) international issues. Place them in an order of priority which the group agrees. When you have finished, share your group's ideas in a class discussion. See if you can reach agreement and draw up a class list of a) national issues and b) world issues in order of priority.

ROLE PLAY

Our daily life and experiences affect the way we see things. As a result, a priority for one person can appear trivial to another.

In groups of six, take one of the following roles:
1) the head of a one parent family
2) a middle-aged person who is married with teenage children
3) a young married person with no children who wants to buy a home
4) an old age pensioner who lives alone
5) a self-employed person who wants to expand their business
6) an unemployed person between 20 and 30

As the person in your role, tell the group why you agree or disagree with the list of priorites drawn up by the class.

■ FOR YOUR FOLDER ■

1 Copy out the lists of priorites drawn up by the class. Write a brief statement saying whether you agree or disagree with these and give reasons for your views.

Or

2 Interview some people from one of the groups listed in the *role play* section above, about their priorities. Then write up a brief article from your findings.

Often in politics, as in your personal life, policies depend on money. If you want to buy something you cannot immediately afford, you have to decide on a policy that will enable you to find the money to do so.

How can I get a personal stereo?

A) Get a part time job
B) Save from spending money
C) Cut down spending on clothes
D) Ask parents for a loan to be repaid from spending money
E) Cut down on nights out with friends

If a government wants to find extra money for one of its priorities, it also has to make a choice between different policies.

How can the government pay for improving the Health Service?

1 Increase its borrowing
2 Budget carefully over the next few years
3 Increase taxation
4 Cut spending on something that's not very important
5 Cut the budget of some other department even though they need the money

IN PAIRS

Try to match the possible policies for increasing spending on the Health Service with the possible ways of raising money for a personal stereo. Once you have matched the policies, discuss how much they are alike.

How the government raises its money

Each year, usually in March or April, the Chancellor presents a plan called the Budget to the House of Commons. In it, the Chancellor explains how much money the Government needs for the following year, and how it intends to raise the money. Some is raised through borrowing. The rest is raised through taxation. So the Budget usually contains proposals to increase or to cut taxes.

Deciding a political policy

This exercise shows you the sort of choices a government has to make when deciding on a particular policy. It shows how a decision on one issue – in this case, spending more on the Health Service – cannot be taken without thinking about other issues.

AIM – To spend more on the health service
Possible courses of action

Increase taxes and:
1 spend it all on health
2 spend it on health and defence
3 spend it on health and education
4 spend it on health and social security and unemployment benefits

Keep taxes as they are and:
5 increase health spending by cutting defence
6 increase health spending by cutting education
7 increase health spending by cutting social security and unemployment benefits
8 increase health spending by trimming all the others

Decrease taxes and:
9 increase health spending by cutting defence
10 increase health spending by cutting education
11 increase health spending by cutting social security and unemployment benefit
12 increase health spending by cutting all the others.

ON YOUR OWN

Study the 12 different policies to increase spending on health. Think about your priorities first, and then choose which policy you would support if you had to make a decision. Write down your reasons.

IN GROUPS

In groups of five discuss the policies you each chose and explain your reasons. Then decide on a policy as a group. Get a spokesperson to explain your group's choice to the class.

NUCLEAR WEAPONS DO WE NEED THEM?

THINKING ABOUT DEFENCE

Britain's defence policy is based on deterrence – that is, the government believes that if we have nuclear weapons, no one will attack us for fear of being attacked in return. Are nuclear weapons a necessary part of our defence policy? What do you think?

YES

"People seem to think that NATO are ready to press the button at the first opportunity. This is not true, NATO was set up after World War II to keep Europe together and maintain American back-up. They're not warmongers. They just believe that you have to appear strong to potential enemies. When you look back at previous wars it's always the weak countries that come under attack. Even Hitler knew better than to invade the stronger nations. He picked on countries like France and Poland who were in no position to fight back. People worry about countries like Libya and Iran, but if they started causing trouble to the West, the last thing we'd want to be is empty-handed.

"We do actually want to get rid of nuclear weapons, but we want multilateral disarmament, where everyone gets rid of their weapons through negotiations and gradual steps. There has to be some means of verification as well, so that we can check that the agreement is being upheld.

"A lot of emphasis is put on the fact that a vast amount of money is being spent on nuclear weapons. But even if we got rid of them we'd still have an arms race, because we'd have to build up our conventional forces, like tanks, because the Soviet Union is stronger on that front too."

Jacci Parnell, a member of Peace through NATO

NO

"The biggest lie is that we need nuclear weapons. There are hundreds of countries who don't have them and they don't have problems. Scandinavia is right next to Russia and they don't feel the need to arm themselves with nuclear weapons. The deterrent doesn't work, because if the button was pressed it would lead to suicide. It would be like mugging someone with a hand grenade. The attacker gets killed too. NATO have said that they will only use their weapons under attack, but how far does it have to go? It's NATO policy to use nuclear weapons against conventional forces. We're led to believe that the Soviet Union has much stronger conventional power than us, but this is a lie. The International Institute of Strategic Studies say there is a conventional balance, so saying we need nukes against Russia's other forces is complete rubbish. It's very frightening. If we carry on it only needs one nuclear conflict to destroy everything and CND won't be around to say, I told you so.

"When you think about it, our so-called deterrent didn't stop Argentina, who didn't have nuclear weapons, from invading the Falklands. This is because they know we won't press the button. The thing is, if we're never going to press the button, as NATO would have us believe, what's the point of having missiles? The money should be used for famine relief and social needs.

Phil Woodford, a member of the Campaign for Nuclear Disarmament

■ THE FACTS ■ ■ ■ ■ ■ ■

- NATO (The North Atlantic Treaty Organisation) was formed in 1949 by 16 countries including most of Europe and the USA. If any of these countries were threatened it would be considered an attack against all of them.

- The Warsaw Pact is an alliance of East European countries and was formed in 1955 in response to NATO. It includes the Soviet Union, Bulgaria, Czechoslovakia, East Germany, Hungary, Poland and Rumania.

- There are enough nuclear weapons to destroy the world many times. Over 500,000 have been built in the last 40 years.

- It is estimated that there are between 200 and 500 British warheads, some of which are based in West Germany.

- There are 1,200 American nuclear weapons based in this country. These are Cruise missiles at Greenham Common and Molesworth.

- In 1987 Britain spent £18,782 million on defence, about 13% of the total budget. Of this, £882 million was on Polaris and Trident nuclear weapons.

- The 1987 treaty between the USA and the USSR is the world's first real disarmament treaty, calling for the withdrawal and destruction of 2,700 land-based intermediate missiles from Europe over three years. This means Cruise and Pershing missiles on the American side and mainly SS20 missiles on the Russian side.

NUCLEAR WEAPONS: AND THE DEFENCE OF BRITAIN

Arguments for nuclear weapons

1 Nuclear deterrence has been a major factor in keeping peace since World War II.

2 Not having nuclear weapons doesn't mean that other countries won't use them against us. We would be wide open to attack.

3 Without nuclear weapons of our own, we wouldn't have a voice in controlling them by multi-lateral disarmament negotiations.

4 We are part of NATO, which must stay evenly matched with the Warsaw Pact countries to keep a balance of power. NATO must have nuclear weapons because the others are vastly ahead in the size of their armed forces and number of conventional weapons.

5 Paying for nuclear weapons is cheaper than building up the stock of conventional weapons. This gives us more to spend on public services and stops bigger increases in taxation.

Arguments against nuclear weapons

1 Having more and more nuclear weapons makes it more likely that a war will start, accidentally or not.

2 If we were fighting a super-power on our own, it would be foolish to use nuclear weapons in the face of their superior power to strike back.

3 Owning our own nuclear weapons, and letting American missiles be placed here, makes Britain a prime target whether we use them first or not.

4 It is insanity to take even the tiniest risk of nuclear war when we all know how terrible the destruction will be. Why increase the risk by having our own nuclear weapons?

5 Many countries do not have nuclear weapons, even though they could easily make them. Some are even members of NATO. They have not been invaded.

KEY WORDS

Conventional weapons – any weapons that are not nuclear weapons.

Multilateral disarmament – the removal of nuclear weapons by a number of countries, all of which have agreed to get rid of them.

Nuclear deterrence – stockpiling nuclear weapons by one country in the belief that this will discourage other countries from attacking it.

Unilateral nuclear disarmament – the removal of nuclear weapons by one country, regardless of what other countries are doing.

IN GROUPS

1 Talk about the arguments for and against the use of nuclear weapons.
2 Which of the arguments for and which against does the group think are the strongest? The weakest?
3 Try to agree on a group statement about the use of nuclear weapons. This must show the feelings of the whole group. If you are divided, then say so in the statement.
4 Is there any other information you wish you had had to help you come to a decision? How could you obtain it?
Share your group statement with the other groups.

FOR YOUR FOLDER

Make up your mind whether, at the present time, you agree or disagree with having nuclear weapons as part of Britain's defence policy. Write a statement explaining your views.

Different political systems
HUMAN RIGHTS

The Universal Declaration of Human Rights, although not legally binding, was signed by all members of the United Nations in 1948. This Declaration is often used by countries to try to prove that their actions are right, or to claim that the actions of another country are wrong. Here is a shortened and simplified list of the main points from the document.

○ *You have the right to life and to live in freedom and safety.*

○ *All rights apply whatever your sex, race, colour, religion, political opinion, wealth or country of origin.*

○ *You have the right to make up your own mind and choose your own religion.*

○ *You have the right to education.*

○ *No one has the right to make you a slave.*

○ *No one has the right to torture you, nor can you torture anyone.*

○ *You have the right to equal treatment by the law.*

○ *You must be presumed innocent until proven guilty.*

○ *You have the freedom to take an active part in your country's affairs.*

○ *You have the right to the highest possible standard of physical and mental health.*

○ *You have the right to work in just and favourable conditions.*

○ *You have the right to be free from unjust interference in family, home, privacy, or correspondence.*

○ *You have the right to come and go in your country, to leave it and to return if you wish.*

○ *You have the right to form groups, including trade unions.*

○ *You have the right to own property.*

○ *Your rights are only limited as far as it is necessary to protect the rights of others.*

○ *You have the right to a decent standard of living.*

○ *You have the right to the benefits of cultural life and scientific progress.*

○ *You have the right to express your thoughts freely through any media, such as books, newspapers, television.*

IN PAIRS

1 Discuss each human right with your partner. Try to agree on what each means.
2 Discuss what would result if each right were taken away.
3 Each of you select seven rights that you think are most important and put them in rank order. Then discuss your list with your partner before coming to a final decision.

CLASS DISCUSSION

1 Produce a large chart and record the top seven rights on each class member's list.
2 Work out from the chart which rights the members of your class think are the most important. Discuss the reasons why the class thinks these are important.
3 Are there any rights not included in the class chart? Discuss why you think these have been left out.

The actions of the USA and USSR are based on different sets of ideas (ideologies). The ideology of the USSR is *communism*. The USA, which is against communism, believes in ideas of *capitalism*. Each side believes it has a better system than the other.

Imagine a debate between a speaker for the communists (USSR) and one for the capitalists (USA). Both believe they hold the truth. Both believe their truth gives the fairest way to govern, to run the economy and the best deal for the people of their society. Here is what they might say.

THE GREAT DEBATE

What about freedom?

'Capitalism is determined to protect the freedom of the individual. This is true in every area of life. Under capitalism the rights and liberties of the individual are safeguarded. Everyone has freedom of choice. The press and TV are free to say what they want. People can go where they like and meet whom they please.'

'Only under communism can the individual be free. Capitalism turns the worker into a wage-slave. Freedom exists only for the rich in capitalist countries. Capitalism gives the rich the freedom to overeat and the poor the right to starve. Real freedom of choice can exist only where people are equal – under communism.'

What about government?

'The best government is the least government. People should be left to get on with their own lives. Government has no right to interfere. There are

strict limits on the power of governments. The people must be given the first say. Government depends on the consent of the people. They must have the right to choose between more than one political party in fair competition in elections. Communist governments seize power for one political party. They turn people into slaves and give them no choice or say in politics.'

'Governments are needed only because of the evil of capitalism. They exist in capitalist countries only to help keep the workers in their place. We need *our* government only to protect our workers from foreign attack. There is no need for more than one party. The Communist Party represents all the workers. Other parties would be reactionary and counter-revolutionary. The Communist Party is the one true voice of the workers.'

What about competition?

'Competition is essential for a healthy society. Capitalism gives the individual the right to compete fairly. The hard-working and the able must be allowed to succeed. Competition makes for efficiency and keeps prices down. Competition is also a fact of life. Human nature is competitive. Without the promise of personal *reward,* people will not work. Unless some

people are allowed to make profits, wealth will not be created for everybody else. Enforced equality means bringing everyone down to the level of the lazy and the feeble.'

'Communism offers an alternative to competition. Society need not be a jungle. In a communist society each individual gives according to his or her ability and receives enough to meet his or her needs. All men and women are equal. Everyone sees the fairness of the system, and rewards are shared out equally. Therefore everyone is willing to work hard to make it better. People cooperate for the common good rather than compete for personal advantage.'

What about the economy?

'The economy is best left to run itself. Individuals have the right to own their own businesses and work for their own profit. Government ought not to interfere. The less restrictions made by government, the better the economy works, and the more profit and wealth are created.'

'The economy must be planned by the state and run for the good of all of the people. Firms cannot be left in the hands of greedy, profit-hungry capitalists. The state must own all resources and businesses and run them for the benefit of the people as a whole.'

IN GROUPS

Study the statements made by the two speakers. Make one list of the capitalist ideas about freedom and government, and another list of the communist viewpoints.

Look again at the list of human rights. Select the five rights that you think will be given the highest priority in a capitalist country, such as the USA, and a communist country, such as the USSR. Make them into two lists and then discuss any similarities and differences.

FOR YOUR FOLDER

Think again about your list of the seven most important human rights. Have you changed your ideas after group and class discussions? Decide on a final list, write it down, and say why you chose these seven rights.

PREPARING YOURSELF: REVISION

Organisation is the key to successful revision

1 Revision should be a continuous process

Students tend to regard revision as something they do – if at all – immediately before exams. But to be effective, revision is best done as a continuous process. If you get into the habit (for your own purposes) of turning all your essays, projects, short- and long-term assignments into simple diagrams, flow-charts and graphs, when the examinations come revision is no more than making sure you can recall the diagrams for the purpose of turning them back into words.

IN PAIRS

1 How far is revision a continuous part of your study programme?
2 Do you attempt to break down your essays and assignments into diagrams or concise notes on revision sheets?

2 Make a revision timetable

As the exam draws near, you will need to be quite organised about your revision. For the final five or six weeks you should work out a revision timetable. Make a list of the topics that have to be revised and decide what order they should be tackled in. Space out the revision for each topic and make a note of what you intend to revise during each day of your revision timetable. To keep up interest it is usually better to revise a variety of topics each day rather than spend all day on just one topic. Don't forget to leave plenty of time for rest and leisure, especially in the last few days before the exam.

IN PAIRS

Each draw up a draft revision timetable for the period immediately before the exams. When you have finished, talk through your timetables and suggest any alterations that you think might improve them.

3 Form a revision group

One very valuable way to revise is to join up with a couple of friends who are doing the same course as you, and meet together two or three times a week to revise topics as a group. Clearly, you need to all get on together, but you must make sure that such revision sessions don't turn into chat sessions!

Working as a group helps you to see the course as a whole. Working by yourself you can be so interested in one area that

you completely miss out other important areas. Within a group, however, other people's likes will probably be different from yours. This means you can help make each other aware of the syllabus as a whole, and of what may come up in the exam.

Also, on account of this difference of interests, members of the group are likely to find themselves 'teaching' the others whenever their special topics come under discussion. And, as all teachers know, the best way to learn something yourself is to teach it to somebody else.

Psychologically also, it is valuable to work as a member of a revision group rather than on your own. Talking to other people can help lessen the anxiety that might otherwise build up.

IN GROUPS

Discuss the idea of forming a revision group. List what you consider would be the advantages and disadvantages of working in a group. On balance, does it strike you as a good way of revising?

4 Find out all you can about the examinations

In order to revise for an exam it should be obvious that you must find out all you can about it. Get hold of a copy of the syllabus: What topics are listed? Look at past exam papers: What sort of questions are asked? Are questions on some topics compulsory? How long do you get to answer each question?

IN PAIRS

Work with a partner who is studying one or two different subjects from you. Each choose a subject that the other is not doing. Get a copy of the syllabus and some past papers and study them. Then, take it in turns to tell each other about the exam in the subject you have chosen.

REVISION SHEETS

You cannot hope to memorise whole essays or passages which are hundreds of words long. You do not need to do so. You can learn more easily and better if you break down the essay or passage into smaller bits. You can do this by making revision sheets using headings, sub-headings and key words and phrases to help you remember what is important.

IN PAIRS

Study the passage below on criminal courts. If you had to know its main points for an exam, how would you attempt to keep them in your mind? Make a revision sheet by writing down notes to help you. (The first paragraph has been done for you, see below and right.)

IN GROUPS

Form groups and compare sheets. Which sheets are the most useful? Why?

Revision sheet

CRIMINAL COURTS
1 Criminal Cases-Mostly Minor (Paragraph heading)
  A) Punishments (Sub heading)
    (i) fines
    (ii) Community service   } Key words
    (iii) Probation   and phrases
    (iv) not more than 3 mths Jail
  B) Magistrates Courts (sub heading)
    (i) Justices of the peace (JP's)
    (ii) Lay (not legally qualified)
    (iii) 18,000 part time   } Key words
    (iv) appointed   and phrases
    (v) nominated by local
         political parties

Your next heading will be paragraph 2 and your next subheading will be C.

Sub heading
Key phrase
Key phrase – part-time
Key word
Key phrase

Paragraph heading
key phrase and words
Sub-heading
key phrase
Key word
Key phrase

Criminal courts

The great majority of criminal cases are relatively minor and carry punishments of fines, community service, probation or at most three months in jail. These come before local magistrates courts which are staffed by unpaid 'lay' Justices of the Peace (JPs). They are described as lay because JPs are not required to be legally qualified. There are about 18,000 JPs, most of whom sit for one or two half-days per week. They are not elected, but appointed by the Lord Chancellor on the advice of local Advisory Committees which work in secret and tend to receive most nominations from local political parties.

The system of appointing JPs has been criticized for being secret and for giving considerable power without public accountability. The ranks of the JPs have also been criticized for being dominated by middle-aged and middle-class males, and local Advisory Committees have been instructed to try for a more balanced social and sexual mix. In some of the larger cities full-time legally qualified magistrates called stipendiaries have been appointed. In addition to minor cases these courts, which never sit with a jury, also hold committal proceedings to establish whether a more serious case appears to exist for referral to the Crown Courts.

Crown Courts are staffed either by judges or by recorders assisted by JPs. A recorder is a practising barrister or solicitor who acts in this capacity part-time and deals with minor cases. The more serious cases are heard by judges who sit with a jury. A jury is a group of 12 ordinary citizens selected at random to hear cases. They are supposed to listen to the cases put by the 'prosecution' which is trying to convict the persons accused of the crimes, and the 'defence' which is trying to prove their innocence. They then have to decide whether the accused are guilty or not. When the jury has reached that decision, which must usually be unanimous (although the judge may accept a majority verdict of 10 to 2), the judge decides the punishment. The right to trial by jury is a long-established custom in English criminal law and relates to the principle of 'trial by equals'.

REVISION STRATEGIES

1 In my revision I try to summarise the topic.

2 During revision I concentrate on one point at a time.

3 When revising I concentrate on learning the facts.

4 When trying to remember something new I link it to something I already know.

5 I revise things by saying them over and over in my head.

6 When revising I concentrate on what I don't know.

7 When revising I consider how the various aspects link together.

8 I try to memorise everything when I revise.

9 After a period of revision, I try to explain to someone else what I have learned.

10 I revise by copying out my essays again.

IN GROUPS

1 Successful revision depends upon using the most suitable strategies, or ways of going about it. Broadly, there are two approaches to revision: *active approaches* which require thought and organisation and *passive approaches* which do not. Study the revision strategies on the left and make them into two lists marked 'Active approach' and 'Passive approach'.

2 An active approach to revising is more likely to be helpful than a passive one. Discuss why this is so.

PROBLEMS WITH REVISION

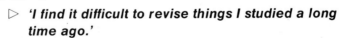

▷ *'I find it difficult to revise things I studied a long time ago.'*

▷ *'I find things I didn't understand originally difficult to revise.'*

▷ *'Subjects with a lot to revise are a problem for me.'*

▷ *'I don't find enough time to revise as much as I need.'*

▷ *'I tend to get muddled when revising topics that are similar.'*

▷ *'When revising I have difficulty in recalling the exact words used.'*

▷ *'After revising something I tend to forget it quickly.'*

▷ *'Often, I don't know whether I have revised a topic fully enough.'*

IN GROUPS

On your own, write down any problems that you have had with revision, and what strategies you have developed, if any, to try to overcome your problems. Then, as a group, discuss in turn each person's problems and the problems listed to the left. Draw up a list of revision problems with suggested strategies to overcome them. Appoint a spokesperson to report your ideas to the rest of the class and share your suggestions in a class discussion.

The trial exams

Self assessment schedule

Use this self-assessment schedule to evaluate your performance in the trial exams. Write your answers on a separate sheet.

1 When you were revising for the trial exams, how did you go about it? Some people have definite plans while others don't. Say what you did.

2 How satisfied were you with the way you organised your revision for the trial exams. In what ways do you plan to do it differently when preparing for the exams in the summer? (Refer back to the Revision Strategies on the opposite page.)

3 It is natural to feel anxious about exams. The important thing is to use this anxiety to make you prepare yourself better. How did you react to feeling anxious, depressed or uncertain when you

were revising? Could you be more constructive? If so, in what ways?

4 Did you do your revision entirely on your own or did you work with a friend or group of friends? How do friends working together help one another?

5 Briefly describe how you tackled the exam papers in the matters of timing, order of questions, selection of questions, planning answers. If you feel you could improve your strategy, say how.

FOR YOUR FOLDER

In groups
Show each other your completed self-assessment schedules and discuss them together. Then each write a short statement for your folder saying what you have learned about how to prepare for exams, and how you plan to prepare for the exams in the summer.

Learning from the trial exams

When you get your papers returned, don't just look at the marks and then put them in your files. Listen carefully when your teachers go over the papers in class, and make notes in the margin of any important points you missed out. Then, while the teacher's comments are still fresh in your mind, use some of your study time to go through the paper again and give some thought to why you made the mistakes you did. In this way you can discover any faults in your study strategies and put them right before it is too late.

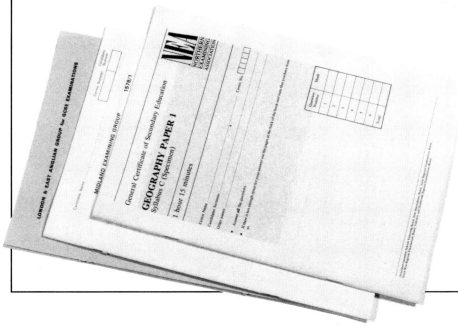

IN PAIRS

Choose a trial exam subject in which you both achieved only average or below average marks. Go through the paper question by question. Compare your answers and discuss them. As you do so, ask yourselves these questions:

- Where did I lose credit?

- Did I get the meaning of the question wrong?

- Did I leave out some important ideas or some good arguments to support the idea?

- Was my answer badly planned or illogical?

- Did I misunderstand some important part of the course?

- Did my memory let me down?

- How would I write my answer if the same question came up again?

- How can I avoid having the same trouble with a similar question in a future exam?

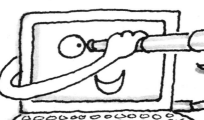

THE DATA PROTECTION ACT

WHAT IS THE DATA PROTECTION ACT?

The Data Protection Act was passed in 1984. Its main provisions came into force in November 1987. The Act gives you the right to know what is being stored about you on computers. It applies to all groups using computers, including the police, schools, hospitals, employers, local authorities, central government and commercial organisations.

WHY IS THE DATA PROTECTION ACT NECESSARY?

More and more organisations are using computers to keep records about you and millions of other people. This sometimes improves services, for instance, in local authority housing departments and X-ray sections of hospitals. It can also help the police to fight crime. But there are dangers in computerising records. Wrong information may be entered or information may be left in after it is out of date. It may get mixed up between two people. The effect can be serious. Individuals can be refused jobs, housing, benefits or credit. They might be overcharged for goods or services. They could even be wrongfully arrested. The Data Protection Act gives you the right to find out what information is being stored about you. It also aims to stop problems like the ones mentioned.

HOW DOES THE DATA PROTECTION ACT TRY TO PROTECT YOU?

There are eight principles which any organisation storing personal information about people on their computers must follow:

1 The information must be collected and used fairly and lawfully.

2 They must register the purposes for which the information is held.

3 The information cannot be used or disclosed except for those purposes.

4 They can only hold information which is related to their purpose, and it cannot be more than is needed.

5 The information they hold must be accurate and, where necessary, kept up to date.

6 The information must not be kept any longer than necessary.

7 Individuals must be allowed to see the information about themselves and, if it is incorrect, to ask for it to be corrected or erased.

8 The proper measures must be taken to ensure that the information does not get into the hands of other people not entitled to know it.

WHAT RIGHTS DOES THE DATA PROTECTION ACT GIVE YOU?

The act gives you five rights:

1 To know if any organisation keeps information about you on computer.

2 To see a copy of the information, except for certain types of information (see 'When can't you see personal details?' right).

3 To make a complaint to the Data Protection Registrar if you don't like the way organisations are collecting or using personal information about you.

4 To have inaccurate records erased or corrected.

5 To claim compensation through the courts if you have been hurt by the loss or destruction of personal data; or through an improper disclosure; or because of inaccuracy.

WHEN CAN'T YOU SEE PERSONAL DATA?

You will not be able to see records about yourself if the data is being held to:
▷ Safeguard national security
▷ Prevent or detect crime
▷ Catch or prosecute offenders
▷ Assess or collect tax or duty

Your right to see health and social services data may also be restricted. Data users do not have to tell you that they are withholding data under one of the above exemptions. They may reply to your enquiry in words like: 'I do not hold any personal data which I am required to reveal to you.' The Act only covers data held on computers, not information held in the ordinary way.

HOW TO USE THE DATA PROTECTION ACT

HOW DO YOU FIND OUT WHO KEEPS WHAT DATA?

Go to the major public library in your neighbourhood. There you will find a copy of the Data Protection Register. The Register lists data and computer bureaux and gives details of:

▷ What sort of data they hold.
▷ The type of data subject (such as employees, customers, voters).
▷ The purposes for which they hold the data.
▷ How they obtain the data.
▷ How they use the data and to whom it will be disclosed.

The register entry also gives an address you can write to with a subject access request.

HOW DO YOU FIND OUT WHAT DATA IS HELD ABOUT YOU?

Write a letter to the data user asking to be supplied with any information that is held about you. See the sample below for the sort of letter you could write.

The data user may reply by sending you a standard form to fill in, and may ask you for a fee. The data user may also ask for additional information from you, or for proof of your identity.

Dear Sir

I wish to make an application under S.21 of the Data Protection Act 1984. Please supply me with any information which you hold about me to which I am entitled.

If you require further information from me or a fee, please let me know as soon as possible.

If you do not normally handle these requests for your organisation, please pass this letter to your Data Protection Officer or other appropriate official.

Yours faithfully

WHAT DO YOU DO IF YOU'RE NOT SATISFIED?

You may not be satisfied for three reasons:

1 You have not been given the information you asked for.

2 You suspect you have not been given all the information you asked for.

3 The information is wrong.

You should first write back to the organisation asking for all the information or for a correction of the mistake.

If the organisation doesn't cooperate, you can either go to court or complain to the Data Protection Registrar. If you go to the county court, the court can ask to see the information and may make an order compelling the data user to remedy any mistake. You can complain to the Registrar by writing to: Investigation Department, Office of the Data Protection Registrar, Springfield House, Water Lane, Wilmslow, Cheshire SK9 5AX.

WHAT POWERS DOES THE REGISTRAR HAVE?

The Registrar will investigate your complaint. If they find they agree with you, they will ask the organisation to correct the mistake or omission. If this does not happen, the Registrar can issue an enforcement notice requiring the data user to put it right. It is a criminal offence to disobey this enforcement notice.

CAN YOU GET COMPENSATION?

If you have suffered damage and distress from the loss, unauthorised destruction or disclosure of information about yourself, or through inaccurate data, you can seek compensation through the courts.

Key words

Data: information recorded on computers, word processors or punched card processors.
Personal data: information about a particular person.
Data subject: an individual about whom personal data is stored.
Data user: a person or organisation who holds and controls personal data.
Subject access request: an enquiry by a person to an organisation to find out if there is computerised data held about them.

ROLE PLAY

'I can't see the point of it'.
In pairs, discuss the purpose of the Data Protection Act and why it needed to be introduced. Then, act out a scene in which someone explains the aims of the Act and its main principles to a friend who has said: 'I can't see the point of it'.

IN PAIRS/GROUPS

Work on your own and produce a diagram or flow chart explaining how to use the Data Protection Act. When you have finished, show your diagram or chart to your partner and the rest of the group. Discuss whose diagram or chart is the most successful and why.

FOR YOUR FOLDER

Write a short statement about the Data Protection Act saying what rights it gives you and why.

You have written to Customer Contact plc, 136 High Street, Northburton NB6 7DZ to enquire whether or not they hold any data about you. They have replied asking for a £10 fee and asking you to provide proof of your identity. Write your reply.

WHOSE GOT A FILE ON YOU?

Many different sorts of organisations store personal information about you. These include police, schools and hospitals, other public agencies

The DHSS

Very little social security information is held on computer but the amount is likely to increase under the DHSS computerisation programme.

Computers are mainly used to print out order books for payments such as pensions and child benefit, or giro cheques for short-term benefits. A typical computer record will contain the name, address and birth date of the applicant and dependants, including the age of children, together with the amount of benefit to be paid. This information will be open to you for checking by applying to a local DHSS office, as will individual National Insurance contribution records. These are already supplied on demand.

Much of the most sensitive information passing through social security offices, such as fraud investigation is not on computer and will therefore not be accessible.

The Home Office

The Home Office stores details of passport applications. It also files all details of people's movements with the new 'machine-readable' passports, which are gradually being introduced. The only grounds for refusing access to these types of files are to ensure national security or for the 'prevention or detection of crime'.

The immigration service also stores data on many thousands of people. If you want to see a personal file held by the immigration service, you should make a written application to the Home Office. They will supply a form asking for a list of the data required and, in some cases, for proof of identity.

The National Health Service

Personal health records can be withheld on the grounds that disclosing information would cause 'serious harm to physical or mental health'. Personal health details are more likely to be held on computer by hospital consultants than GP.

GPs, however, have computer systems for their patient registration records and for call-up systems such as repeat prescriptions or required checkups, and these should be open to access.

Family practitioner committees also hold information on computer starting with the patient register which gives the name, previous names, address, date of birth and NHS number. There are no medical details.

If you want access, you will normally apply to the health authority or family practitioner committee concerned as 'data user', although GPs have to register individually for their own computers and deal with direct applications.

The information will then be sent to you, or more likely an appointment may be arranged in order to give an explanation and any counselling which may be thought necessary.

Social Services Department

Social work records, like personal health records, can be withheld on the grounds that disclosure might cause 'serious harm' – to the data subject or anyone else – or that access would be likely to give away the identity of a third person to whom the information also relates, or who may have supplied it. The decision whether or not to withhold information will be taken by a senior officer. Guidelines state that withholding information on grounds of serious harm should be 'most exceptional' but could apply in cases of mental disorder or risk of child abuse. Voluntary organisations which may hold personal data on computer, such as the NSPCC and private care homes, have similar guidelines.

Security Service and the Special Branch

The Security Service and the Special Branch are exempted from the Data Protection Act. They do not have to reveal what information they hold on you on the grounds that it could be a danger to national security.

The Inland Revenue and the Customs and Excise

The Inland Revnue stores information about people for the purposes of collecting tax, and the Customs and Excise department for collecting VAT. They do not have to register under the Data Protection Act and do not have to reveal what information they hold about you.

Educational establishments

Schools, colleges and universities all keep personal and academic records. Schools normally keep records on your background, medical history, learning progress (including the results of any tests/continuous assessment) and dealings with educational psychologists or welfare officers. But since the Act only applies to computerised records, and most school records are still kept manually, you are not entitled to check them.

The police

All police forces in the UK have had to register with the Data Registrar. You have a right to ask your local force whether they are keeping any information about you on their force computer system or on the Police National computer.

A standard application form has been produced by the Association of Chief Police Officers. This can be obtained by post or by calling at local police stations.

Depending on the type of information you require, you will have to provide certain facts to establish your right to the confidential information. The police will require your title, name, former name, sex and in certain sensitive categories your place of birth, height and other identification items.

There are seven separate categories of information on the police national computer. You will be asked to select which categories you want. You can ask for all seven categories to be searched but each search will cost £10, or £70 for the lot.

The seven categories are: crime pattern analysis of major incidents where any name that is included is only incidental; criminal names and criminal convictions with a cross reference to the card index system which is also in the process of being put on computer; fingerprints; disqualified drivers; wanted or missing persons; a vehicle index which includes registration numbers, owners and stolen or suspect vehicles; a message log which records all PNC (police national computer) inquiries.

You also have a right to know what information the police force is keeping about you on its own computer system. These categories vary from force to force but include registers of major crimes, criminal records, firearms registers, burglar alarm systems plus up to another 10 categories. You have a right to know about the categories and can again ask for a search of each at a cost of £10 per category.

Under the law the police are exempted from releasing details if doing so would hamper them in preventing or detecting crime or catching or prosecuting offenders.

Financial Organisations

Organisations such as credit reference agencies, banks, finance houses, credit card companies, insurance companies, even department stores and mail order companies, have personal financial records stored on computer. The Data Protection Act gives you the right to demand to see details of your personal finance files, but the financial network is very complex. Most financial institutions, and even some banks, swap personal finance files. If a piece of false information about you gets fed into one of the files, it may get transferred onto several others. It can be very difficult to track down where the mistake was made and have it corrected on all the files on which it is held.

IN GROUPS

Discuss these statements:

1   'Parents and children should have the right to see everything that is stored on school files, whether it is on a computer or in a manilla folder.'

    What do you think?

2   'Doctors shouldn't have the right to withhold medical information from you. It's your body. You should know everything about it.'

    'I don't think so. It's right that doctors should make the decision what to tell their patients. After all, they are the experts, not you.'

    What do you think?

3   'It is ridiculous that you should have to pay £70 to find out what data the police are holding about you on the police national computer.'

    'No it isn't. If you didn't have to pay, they'd get so many enquiries they wouldn't be able to cope with them.'

    What do you think?

4   'It strikes me that there are so many exemptions, it's so expensive to make an enquiry, and it's hard to track down wrong information that the Data Protection Act is a toothless tiger.'

    'Whatever its weaknesses, the Data Protection Act is a step in the right direction.'

    What do you think?

5   What changes, if any, do you think would improve the Data Protection Act?

FOR YOUR FOLDER

Write a statement saying how you feel about having many organisations hold personal data about you. Do you think the computer revolution has benefitted us greatly by making it so much easier for organisations and government departments to keep track of us as individuals? Or do you feel that is an infringement of your liberty that so many people hold information about you, not all of which you have access to?

Equality for women?

The two pictures show women in Britain in 1912 and 1988. Acts of Parliament between these dates have given women the vote and made sexual discrimination illegal at work and in many other areas of life. The battle for equal rights by women has been a long one. Has it finally been won?

EQUAL PAY?

To the right is a graph comparing the hourly pay of male and female manual workers from 1970 to 1984. The rates shown are those earned in pence per hour by male manual workers. The rate given for females is shown as a percentage of this rate.

Men	54.6p per hour	61.2p per hour	63.6p per hour	78.6p per hour	90.1p per hour			338p per hour	367p per hour	Men
Women	59%	60%	65%	61%	64%			71%	70%	Women
	1970	1971	1972	1973	1974	1975		1983	1984	

1975 saw the introduction of the Equal Pay Act that made it illegal to pay a woman less than a man if she does the same or a similar job.

GROUP DISCUSSION

1 Are you surprised that, since the Equal Pay Act, the improvement in women's wages compared to men's is only about 6%? Can you think of any ways that an employer can get round the Act (for example, what is the difference between a cleaner and a janitor)? Has the fact that a woman's wage is often a 'second wage' anything to do with women accepting this lower rate? Do you think that women will ever get equal pay in manual jobs? Do you think they should get equal pay?

2 Discuss the following statements:

'Men are the main wage earners in most cases and should earn more than women.'

'Women get other perks such as time off to have children and a guaranteed job to come back to.'

'Men ought to get more because they don't leave to raise a family.'

'Of course women should get the same wage if they are doing the same job as a man.'

'In manual jobs a woman can't do as much as a man because she isn't as strong. So she should get paid less.'

EQUALITY OF OPPORTUNITY?

Since 1975 advertisements like the following have become illegal.

RESPONSIBLE LADY required to act as secretary to a small board of directors. Apply giving full details of experience to PO Box 777X.

BOYS with six or more 'O' levels needed by various firms to train as engineers.

Apply in the first instance to Agency, 44B The Mall, Glasgow.

Experienced men are wanted as part of an expanding sales team.
Salary is negotiable between £10,000 and £12,500.
Ring 01 666 7893

Waitresses required three evenings per week. Rate of pay, £1.50 per hour. Apply The Hop, Breslaw Street, Higherford after 6 pm.

IN GROUPS

Discuss whether you think that advertisements like the examples should be banned by law.

Your discussion may include some of the following points:

Is it unreasonable for a board of directors to want a female secretary, or a publican to want women to wait on customers? Can you think of any reasons why women are preferred for these jobs? Are these reasons good enough to allow advertisements like the examples?

Is it fair that only men are wanted for a sales team and boys to train as engineers? If the employers want males, why should they not be allowed to advertise for them?

Rewrite the advertisements in a form that does not include any sexual discrimination.

IN PAIRS

The examples of advertisements from pre-1975 also bring out another factor about equality of opportunity: that of 'male' and 'female' jobs. For example, in mechanical engineering, of the 76,000 women employed in 1985, nearly 70% were either administrative, or clerical staff.

With your partner make a list of the jobs that you think are 'traditionally' for men and those that are 'traditionally' for women.

Go through your lists and try to decide whether you think there are any jobs at all that should be restricted to one sex or the other.

CLASS DISCUSSION

Share your decision about whether there should be any restrictions on jobs with the rest of the class. What are the jobs, if any, that people think women should not or could not do? Are these jobs considered wrong for women only because they require physical strength, or are there any other reasons? Do you think allowances should be made for differences in physical strength? What are the jobs, if any, that people think men should not or could not do? What are the reasons for the choice(s)?

EQUALITY AT WORK AND IN PROMOTION?

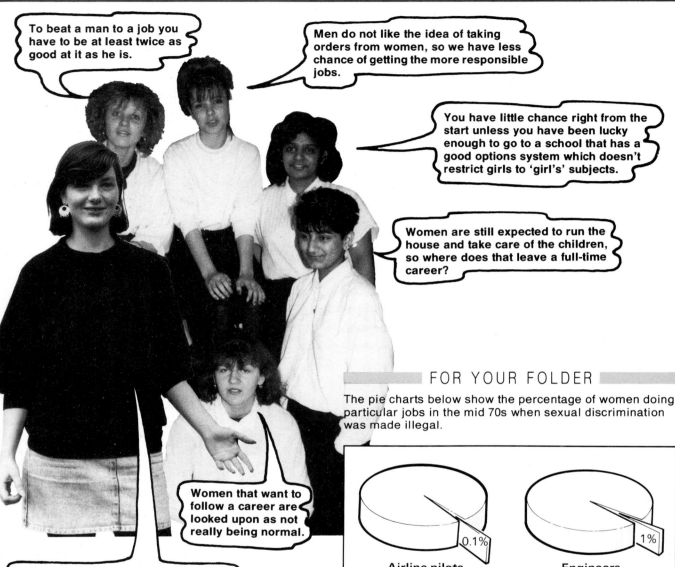

To beat a man to a job you have to be at least twice as good at it as he is.

Men do not like the idea of taking orders from women, so we have less chance of getting the more responsible jobs.

You have little chance right from the start unless you have been lucky enough to go to a school that has a good options system which doesn't restrict girls to 'girl's' subjects.

Women are still expected to run the house and take care of the children, so where does that leave a full-time career?

Women that want to follow a career are looked upon as not really being normal.

Men don't like employing women as their equals because they are so used to bossing their wives around at home.

FOR YOUR FOLDER

The pie charts below show the percentage of women doing particular jobs in the mid 70s when sexual discrimination was made illegal.

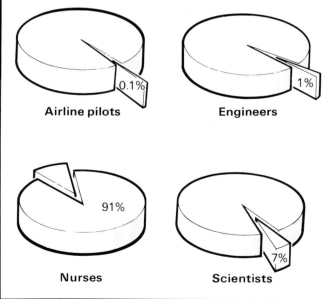

Airline pilots — 0.1%

Engineers — 1%

Nurses — 91%

Scientists — 7%

IN GROUPS

Talk about:

1 Do you think that women have less chance of getting a job or promotion because of the reasons given above?

2 Do you think that any of the statements above are good reasons for employing or promoting a man rather than a woman?

3 Are there any other reasons you can think of that may be given as excuses for employing a man rather than a woman?

4 Do you think the laws introduced in 1975 are preventing discrimination against women?

What do you think these figures are now? Give your reasons. Then, do some research to find out what the percentages really are and compare them with your guess.

CENSORED?

WHAT ABOUT PAGE THREE?

In 1986 and 1988 Labour MP Clare Short tried to introduce
a bill in parliament to ban Page Three girls.
She believes that such pictures degrade women, encourage men to
see them as sex objects and may provoke violent sex attacks.

Should Page Three girls bare all or be banned?

For some women topless pin-up girls are the ultimate insult. To others they're just harmless fun. So do these models really affect men's attitudes to women?

Clare Short's main objection is that Page Three exploits *all* women, not just the models themselves. "They're being used, but at the same time they're doing damage to the interests of women more widely," she says. "These pictures create a culture around men which says that women are available for sex, to be lusted after and grabbed at".

Boys growing up with Page Three see an atmosphere where people like Samantha Fox and Maria Whittaker are not only acceptable, but idolised. They are living in a world where a woman's bra capacity matters more than that of her brain. And while women are seen as objects whose primary function is the projection of sex, they will never achieve true equality in matters like employment and pay, says Clare Short. "Page Three is symbolic. If we can ban it it will send out messages to everyone." She feels that the presence of topless girls in daily papers may have contributed to men adopting an excessively macho role. The pin-ups commonly plastered over workplace walls and discussions over the models' merits create an atmosphere that encourages men to make sexual comments to women workers or even, in some cases, to touch them. "I think men have to pretend to be turned on by Page Three so that they feel properly male", says Ms Short.

She believes that the attitude towards women created by Page Three has a direct effect on the number of sex crimes against women. And although there's no scientific evidence to support her, there have been recent cases in which rapists have been found in possession of pin-ups. "These pictures are linked to a distorted view of sexuality which is in turn linked to sexual attacks, rape and all the rest of it," she says.

WHAT A MODEL SAYS

Denice Berry is a glamour model. Here are her views:

What did you think of the campaign in the House of Commons to ban Page Three?
I think it's so hypocritical for these MPs to criticise Page Three, when they're responsible for so many of the terrible things on the other pages.

There's such a lot of things going on in the world which are bad, a picture of a girl topless seems insignificant.

It's just a bit of fun.

Do you agree with the view that it degrades women?
No. People take it much too seriously. Girls walk about topless on the beach, Bo Derek romps naked with a gorilla in *Tarzan*. It's no big deal. It's not so long since women were afraid to show their ankles, and in ten years' time we'll probably think of topless modelling as we do now about women showing their ankles a hundred years ago.

What about the more serious suggestion, that the image of a topless model can contribute to the motives behind rape?
I don't think it can, I really don't. I think that for a man to be capable of raping a woman he's got to be a little bit crazy anyway. So if they can say that it was Page Three that made them do it, then I think they'd always try to blame something else if it was banned.

IN PAIRS ══════════

Study the views given on this page.
Make a list of:
a) the arguments put forward against
   Page Three girls by Clare Short;
b) the arguments in defence of Page
   Three by the model.
   Which of the arguments do you
find the most convincing? Why?
   Each prepare a short speech giving
your views on the Page Three
controversy.

CLASS DEBATE ══════════

Organise a formal debate on the
motion: 'This class believes that daily
newspapers should not be allowed to
publish pictures of topless or nude
models.'

▉ FOR YOUR FOLDER ▉

Write a statement summarising your
views on the Page Three controversy.

Problem page

> Dear Gloria,
>   I've been unemployed for a year. Now I've been offered work as a glamour model. I'm worried about topless and nude modelling. What do you think I should do?
> Nadia

IN PAIRS ══════════

Draft a reply to Nadia. Then, join up
with another pair. Compare replies.

INDUSTRY, PROFITS, PRICES & YOU

Whether a business is a large company employing thousands of workers or a small shop or service run by just one self-employed person, they have to operate in the same way. Both must work out what all their costs are and fix the price of their product(s) or service(s) so that they can make a profit.

IN PAIRS

Read Kim's story and make a list of all the reasons why Kim's business is a success.

IN GROUPS

To start your own business, you would need to work out a plan in order to check that there would be a demand for your product or service and that you would be able to make a profit.

Think of a business idea of your own or choose one of the following ideas: a service such as gardening, painting and decorating; car washing; organising children's parties; selling a product such as greeting cards, wooden toys, soft toys, pottery, wood carvings, candles.

Reread *Kim's Story* and then work out a business plan:

- Who would your customers be?
- How would you find them?
- How much money would you need to start?
- What essential equipment would you require?
- What premises would you need?
- What would your average weekly costs be?
- How many customers would you need in order to break even? To make a profit?

Kim had always been good with dogs. At the age of 15 she got a summer job working in a kennel. She learned how to groom and clip the different breeds, and which tools you need. Although she enjoyed the work, she never seriously considered it as a permanent job, because the pay was very low and you had to live in.

When she left school at 17, she went to college but didn't like it there. So she went on a government training scheme, first working in a clothes shop, then helping at a school with a reception class. It was while she was at the school that she got the idea of trying to set up her own business doing dog grooming and clipping.

Raising the money

"My Afghan hound, Lucinda, had seven puppies, and I sold them for £700. I don't think I could do that again – I worry too much about what sort of homes they're going to. I could never make a business of breeding and selling dogs. Anyway, after paying the stud fee and the vet's bills and all the food for the puppies until they were sold, I was left with about £500 profit. For £200 I bought an old car, a Cortina – it's a saloon car and ideally I could do with an estate car – but this one was going cheap and it hasn't let me down so far. I wanted a car because I thought an important service to offer was to collect and deliver the dogs to and from people's homes. Then I had to tax the car, and pay for the insurance, which was about £100 as I was only 18. The equipment – well, the clippers alone cost £150, but I got them on HP – I just paid the deposit out of my profit from selling the puppies. The rest of

£ IN		£ OUT	
Sold puppies	700	Stud fees	100
		Vet's fees	25
		Food	75
		Car	200
		Tax/Ins.	100
		Equipment	150
TOTAL	700	TOTAL	650

Starting out

ANNABEL COLLIER

RUNNING YOU!
Kim

the stuff wasn't too expensive – combs, scissors, sprays, shampoos. I've got the right stuff, but I still haven't got all the equipment I'd really like.

A supplementary job

For about a year I had a part—time job in a cake shop, working mornings from 9 till 11 to earn a bit of money, because I realised that I wouldn't earn enough from the business at first. It gave me every afternoon to work with dogs, which was fine at the time. I left that a couple of months ago because I wanted to give the business a go full-time. But it didn't really take off to that extent, so a couple of weeks ago I got another

WN BUSINESS:
tory

part-time job working in a newsagents from 6 am to 9 am – that's their busiest time of the day, batching up the papers for the rounds, and people coming in on their way to work to buy papers and cigarettes and sweets. I get £25 a week for that, cash in hand, and I have a lot more time in the day for the dogs so it's better than taking up the whole morning in the cake shop.

Advertising
When I first decided to set up my own business, I put an advert in the local paper: 'Dog clipping and grooming – all breeds catered for – very low prices' – just to see how it would go. And I got quite a good response, considering the advert only cost about £3.

How I decided on my prices? I phoned round other places pretending I had a dog that needed clipping, to find out what they charged. There's a lot of competition so I made sure to fix my prices lower than other people's.

After the first advert, I advertised quite a lot more, and even got a few leaflets printed when business was falling off. My mother and I put the leaflets together ourselves using Letraset and typing – that was this year. The thing was, there was this new petshop opening in Trowbridge doing professional grooming, so I thought if I lowered my prices for a while and put out this leaflet saying 'Special Offer for June', and the prices were lower than the new petshop, it might help. I got about 100 leaflets photocopied and I went round delivering them myself – there are some big housing estates round our way. If you walk up the path and a dog starts barking, you know to put one of your leaflets through the door – otherwise don't bother! Of course, not all dogs bark when someone comes to the door, but it does save you from wasting leaflets otherwise.

Raising a bank loan
When I first started, I was grooming the dogs in our garage. After a couple of months, I thought 'I really must get a shed.' I looked around at various ones, and I saw one that would just suit me nicely – it had windows in and it was just the right size. It was £150, and I didn't have enough, so I just went to the bank and asked for a bank loan. I told them all about the business – they didn't ask to see any paperwork – and I told them what I wanted it for, and they lent me the £100 I asked for. They were really helpful. As I was 18, I didn't have to have anyone to back me for the loan, I got it in my own right.

Building up orders
I've got quite organised now. I keep a box file with pieces of paper with the names and addresses of every customer, and their phone number, and notes about the dog – like whether to get a muzzle ready if it's snappy, or whether to use a dry shampoo if it can't stand the hair-dryer – you can't send them home dripping wet, they look terrible! A few weeks ago I phoned up a lot of people on my books and said 'I'm getting booked up for Christmas, would you like me to fit your dog in?' I made out like I was just phoning them because they were good customers and I didn't want to have to turn them away if I got too booked up, and most of them said 'Oh, yes please, I'd forgotten to phone you' – because they'd been so busy planning for Christmas. I can do four or five dogs in a day, and at the moment I'm so booked up I'd find it hard to fit in any more.

£ IN	£ OUT
Part-time at the cake shop £17.50 p.w.	Advert in paper £3.00
Part-time at the newsagent £25.00 p.w.	Leaflets photocopied £8.00
	Shed £150.00
Payments received per dog £3.50 each	More equipment (grooming table) £75.00
Bank loan £100.00	Car repairs and petrol £60.00
	£296.00 In business!

Running the business

£ IN	
5 dogs per day @ £3.50 each = £17.50	
per week = £17.50 × 5	£87.50
Job at newsagent = £25.00	
Total per week £113.00	

£ OUT	
Repay bank loan (incl. interest)	£10.00
Petrol, heat, light, etc	£12.00 app.
Equipment & supplies	£6.00 app.
Telephone	£4.00 app.
Anything else	£10.00 app.
	£42.00

Balance per week 113.50
− 42.00
PROFITS = 71.50

Making it pay

SPECIALISATION

The ways that people earn their living today, especially in industrialised countries, are too numerous to list. They often specialise in one or even a very small part of a production process. Two hundred years ago, this way of working was unknown. Most people worked on the land and had to grow or make most of the things that they required. Their standard of living remained low because they could not produce more than the bare requirements for each day. The move towards making or working on one thing meant that more of that thing could be produced. It could then be exchanged for the necessary items, which others had produced, and any extra or surplus could be used to acquire some luxuries.

IN PAIRS

Look at the illustrations above. Discuss what the man and woman are each doing or making in the pictures. What else might they produce for themselves from the land?

ON YOUR OWN

Imagine that you had to be self-sufficient by doing everything for yourself, in your house and on the car. Make a list of the things at which you think you would be good, and a list of things which you would find difficult.

IN GROUPS

Imagine you are a group of people who have got together to do all the jobs around each other's houses and cars normally done by mechanics, plumbers, decorators, builders, electricians, etc. Using your individual lists as a guide:

1 Decide what job or jobs each person would be best at doing for your group.

2 Find out if there are any jobs that no one in the group would be able to do.

Compare the results of your investigations with the other groups. Are there any other jobs that could not be done by your group, but that another group could do? Are there any jobs your group could do for another group?

CLASS DISCUSSION

'Specialisation means that making or working on one thing allows more of that thing to be produced.' Explain this statement, saying why you think it is so and giving examples of how it works. (Read the text on page 59 to help you.) Then think about and list any disadvantages you think specialisation has, as compared with working on a wide variety of tasks. Think about this for the individual, a business and the nation.

IN GROUPS

We take many things for granted today as part of everyday life, such as the telephone, cars, cookers, television. Discuss what would probably disappear from the market place if manufacturing were not divided into many small parts, each part requiring a different simple skill.

Would the products that could still be made be the same price as they are today? If not, why? Could the country carry on as it is at the moment if we had to rely on individual people having all the skills required to make a product? Give reasons.

THE DIVISION OF LABOUR

THE DIVISION OF LABOUR

A system in which workers perform a few specialised tasks and then exchange their surplus goods and services is known as the division of labour.

This division of labour is an efficient way of producing goods and services because groups of workers sharing out the different tasks can produce goods at a lower cost than one person trying to do everything. Also, the goods can be produced more quickly and specialist equipment can be in constant use, rather than lying idle while an individual worker moves from one task to the next.

Without the division of labour, it would be impossible to produce complex modern products such as washing machines and refrigerators quickly and cheaply, in large numbers.

IN GROUPS

Manufacturing picture postcards
Work in groups of four. You are aiming to make as many postcards as you can in 20 minutes by sticking photos cut from magazines onto card or A4 paper.

Materials and equipment: You will need copies of old magazines, card or A4 paper, rulers and pencils, scissors and glue.
Production planning: You have 5 minutes to decide on a production plan.
Card specifications: Your customers have specified that each card should measure 10cm x 15 cm.

At the end of the 20 minutes, each group exchange ideas with the class. Explain how your group organised its production. Do you think your organisation was efficient or inefficient? How many cards did you produce? Were they of a satisfactory quality? How could your production methods be improved?

Were there any drawbacks of such a method of production from your viewpoint as workers?

What equipment and reorganisation of the group would you require for mass production of picture postcards?

FOR YOUR FOLDER

Think of six people in your school who do *different* jobs. Write a job description for each of the six and explain how the school illustrates the division of labour.

Are these workers all doing specialised tasks?

HEALTH and SAFETY at WORK

Accidents at work

Every year about 600 people are killed in accidents at work. A further 12,000 people are injured, and about 400,000 people are off work for more than three days because they were hurt at work.

Around 900 people die from work-related diseases each year. Accidents occur at all kinds of workplaces, not just high-risk areas such as building sites. About 40% of serious accidents happen to people working in the service industries such as the health service.

Joan's story

JOAN suffered burns and minor lung damage in a workplace fire that killed several of her workmates. These workers made cuddly toys on the top floor of a three-storey Victorian building. The fire started downstairs in cardboard boxes and waste stacked in a corridor, and the women were caught upstairs. Fire fighters described the top-floor workshop as a 'death trap'. There was no fire escape and the windows had steel bars across them to prevent burglary. Joan was lucky. The fire fighters cut through the bars and got her out. Although the physical injuries she received weren't bad, Joan has suffered from anxiety since the horror of the fire and has been unable to go back to work.

Mary's story

MARY is partially disabled following a serious injury at work. She has had to retire from her job as a nursery nurse on medical grounds. She was asked to move a climbing frame which folded up on her. It was as big as she was. While doing so, a vertebra snapped and a couple of discs in her lower back were crushed. Mary had to spend six weeks in bed and was then admitted to hospital for another four weeks.

Before her accident, Mary had said it was dangerous for one person to move the frame. She had pointed out to her supervisor that, in her previous posts, it was standard safety practice to have two people to move the same sort of frame. Even though her supervisor knew she had a back problem, she was told that there weren't always two staff available to move the frame.

Rights and responsibilities

The Health and Safety at Work Act (1974) lays down what the duties of employers and workers are.

Duties of employers
The main duty of an employer is to 'ensure, so far as is reasonably practicable, the health, safety and welfare at work of all their employees.'

- *The employer must provide workplaces, machines and methods of work that are safe and without risks to health. Proper guards must be fitted to dangerous machinery and machines must be serviced regularly and kept in good working order.*
- *The employer must ensure that machines and chemicals are used, stored and transported safely and without risks to health.*
- *The employer must provide employees with as much information, training and supervision as is necessary to ensure their health and safety.*
- *The employer must provide a safe workplace with safe entrances and exits.*
- *The employer must provide a written safety policy and bring it to the notice of all employees.*

- *The employer must provide a safe and healthy workplace with good welfare facilities and maintain it properly. The workplace must have adequate heating (the minimum temperature for workplaces is 16°C), lighting and ventilation and must not be overcrowded. Welfare facilities – toilets and washrooms – must be provided.*
- *The employer must ensure that their firm's activities do not place the health or safety of any of the general public at risk, for example, from noise, dust or fumes.*

Duties of workers:
As an employee, you must:
- Take reasonable care to avoid injury to yourself or your workmates.
- Follow the health and safety regulations that apply to your workplace.
- Cooperate with your employer to do everything possible to make your workplace safe.
- Behave in a sensible manner at all times and not misuse anything that is provided to make your work safe.

IN PAIRS

Study the drawing of the office. List all the safety hazards. You should find at least 20.

IN GROUPS

1 Discuss Joan's story then Mary's story, answering these questions about each:
   What appears to have been the cause of the accident?
   Was it the employer, the employee, or both who failed to carry out their responsibilities as set out in the Health and Safety at Work Act?
   What lessons can be learned from each case? How could a similar accident be avoided in the future?
2 Make lists of the potential hazards in each of the following workplaces: a canteen; a toy shop; a furniture warehouse; an electrical workshop; a hotel.

FOR YOUR FOLDER

Choose one of the classrooms in your school or college. List the alterations which would be needed in order to make it into an office for six to eight people, each with a word processor and a telephone on their desks, their own filing cabinet and some shelving for them to share for books, box files, etc. Make sure that each person has sufficient lighting and adequate space. (There must be at least 3.7 square metres per person.) Draw a floor plan of the room showing how you would arrange it so that it would be a safe workplace. Indicate where the furniture, power points, electric flexes and telephone cables would go.

The main causes of accidents at work include:

- Lack of training and information on hazards.
- Poor supervision, often geared to keeping the work going rather than safety.
- Unsafe design of workplace and machinery.
- Irregular and poor maintenance of equipment and plant.
- Inadequate testing of chemicals.
- Stress due to poor working conditions or pressure of work.
- Haste due to bonus rates that don't take safety properly into account.
- Failure to analyse illness or accident patterns and detect hazards.

SAFETY ON THE ROADS:

Motorbikes

If you ride a motorbike, you are in more danger than anyone else on the road. Here are some facts about road deaths and serious injuries in 1985. For these statistics, 'motorcyclists' include riders of motorbikes, mopeds and scooters, and their passengers.

15-19 age group
▷ Motorcyclists made up 52% of the total deaths (9% were passengers).

All age groups
▷ Motorcyclists made up 24% of total deaths (2% were passengers).

▷ Car users made up 38% of total deaths.

▷ Pedal cyclists made up 8% of total deaths.

▷ Teenage motorcyclists made up more than 50% of all motorcycle deaths and injuries. They are *three times* more likely to suffer death or injury than motorcyclists in their late thirties.

▷ 44% of motorcyclists in their early twenties who were killed or injured were above the legal limit of alcohol for driving. For all age groups this figure was about 30%.

'Teenagers have a different attitude from older people towards road safety.'

'Teenagers are more likely to drink and ride than older people.'

'The figures are high because there are more teenagers using motorbikes than other age groups.'

'Older people have fewer accidents because they are more experienced road users.'

'Teenagers often ride without the proper gear because they can't afford it.'

'Teenagers don't maintain their motorbikes as well as others.'

'Teenagers have accidents because they often ride bikes that are too powerful for them.'

IN PAIRS

1 Discuss what the poster (on the left) means when it says 'the right gear'. How does each item protect the motorcyclist? In what type of situation is each one important?
2 Another safety campaign for all motorists asked drivers to 'drive defensively'. Discuss what you understand this to mean.

IN GROUPS

1 Look at the figures given (on the left, below) for road accidents of all age groups for motorcyclists, car users and pedal cyclists. In 1985 there were over 10 times more cars on the road than motorcycles, and probably a similar number of pedal cycles. Discuss why, then, the percentage of deaths and serious injuries for motorcyclists of all ages was so high.
2 Why do you think that the death and serious injury rates for teenage motorcyclists are so much higher than for the population as a whole? (Consider the quotes on p. 62.)

The causes of motorcycle accidents

Motorcycle accidents are caused by:

▷ Drinking and riding.

▷ Going too fast for the traffic conditions.

▷ Handling the machine badly and losing control – especially on wet and icy roads.

▷ Making mistakes when turning or overtaking.

▷ Riding with a heavily tinted or a scratched visor.

▷ Many motorcycle accidents are caused by other drivers. Motor-cycles are often hard to pick out at junctions, roundabouts and in heavy traffic, especially at night. Also, when drivers pull out to overtake a vehicle, they sometimes fail to see a motorcyclist because he/she is in their blind spot.

CLASS DISCUSSION

The law making seat belts compulsory for front seat car users has reduced deaths and serious injuries in car accidents. A similar law requiring crash helmets for motorcyclists has had much less effect. Why do you think this is so?

Making the roads safer

What can be done to make our roads safer? Here are some suggestions:

▷ *Lower the speed limits.* A study showed that a pedestrian hit by a car moving at 34 mph has a one in two chance of being killed. If the car is travelling at over 40 mph, there is a nine in 10 chance of being killed.

▷ *Fit tamper-proof controls* to all cars to prevent them from exceeding the speed limit.

▷ *Fit warning devices* in cars, both inside and outside, to warn its driver and other drivers when the speed limit is being exceeded.

▷ *Limit the size, power and speed of motorcycles.* It is the larger, more powerful machines that cause more and worse accidents.

▷ *Introduce a graded driver's licence system for motorcyclists.* Under this system you would have to have a good record of riding smaller machines before you could get a licence for a more powerful one.

▷ *Encourage more people to use public transport.* Buses cause far fewer casualties than cars or motor cycles do.

▷ *Design residential areas where pedestrians are given more importance than cars.* In Holland and Scandinavia there are residential areas with very low speed limits and ramps. Parking spaces are located some distance from housing.

▷ *Pay local authorities for cutting down accidents.* The Department of Transport could give money to any local authority which reduces the number of road deaths and injuries over the year before.

Does the increasing number of vehicles on the roads necessarily make driving less safe?

IN GROUPS

Discuss the suggestions above for making the roads safer, and any other suggestions of your own. Produce a group statement saying what measures you think could be introduced to make our roads safer.

FOR YOUR FOLDER

'The road casualty figures are too high. We should be prepared to have more restrictions in order to save lives.' List the restrictions you would be prepared to agree to in order to save lives.

Planning a family

Deciding whether or not to have children and when to try to have them is one of the most important decisions a couple has to take. Being a parent lasts for life. It can bring lots of pleasure, but it also brings many responsibilities and usually changes the way people live.

IN PAIRS

Discuss and make a list of what rearing a child can mean to parents. What restrictions does it place on their lives? What demands on their time does it make? What responsibilities does it bring? What money problems may be created? What emotional problems may arise? What happens to daily routines?

We knew that a child would cut down our social life. We had to be sure we were ready to accept this.

Bringing up a child can be very expensive. We had to be sure that we would be able to provide for it and ourselves.

CLASS DISCUSSION

Share your views in a class discussion.
What do you think is the major sacrifice or the main responsibility that parents undertake when they decide to have children? Is there a general class agreement or are there many different ideas?

IN GROUPS

1 Pleasures of parenthood
If having children meant only sacrifices and more responsibility, many of us would not be here today. There are many pleasures in parenthood.

Talk about the pleasures of being a parent of a child from babyhood to five. How can we know we are going to love someone we have not even seen? What are the things that children do that give pleasure? Are the pleasures they give different at different ages? Can you feel the same pleasure in another person's child?

Try to come to a group decision on the pleasures of parenthood and share this with the other groups in your class.

2 'It's best to have your family when you're young. The smaller the age gap, the easier it is for you to understand your children and to get along with them.'

'I disagree. It's best to get yourself established as a couple and make sure you've got a home and are right for each other before you start a family.'

Discuss these two views. What do you think is the best age to start a family?

3 'I wouldn't want to have children. They are too much of a responsibility. Besides, I want to lead my own life rather than be tied down by having to look after children.'

Discuss this teenager's point of view.

4 List all the reasons you can think of why some people decide not to have children.

FOR YOUR FOLDER

Write about what you feel a couple should think about when deciding whether or not to have a child.

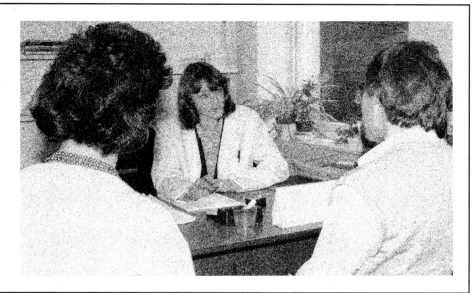

Why can't we have a baby?

Most couples who want to start a family are able to do so. But there are over a million couples who cannot have children even though they would like to. There are many different causes for the inability to have a baby.

In some cases it is the woman who is infertile. For example, there may be a blockage of the fallopian tubes, which prevents the egg from reaching the uterus. Or the ovary may not be producing ripe eggs. In other cases, it is the man who is infertile. He may not be producing enough sperm for some reason.

These are not the only causes. The couple may simply not be having intercourse at the time of the month when ovulation, or the production of eggs, occurs in the woman. There may be psychological factors. For example, a woman who is tense and distressed because she has been unable to conceive is unlikely to become pregnant until she relaxes.

Both men and women can be having difficulties, so if a couple are trying for a baby without success, it is important for both partners to seek medical advice.

IN GROUPS

Some childless couples are so keen to have children that they are prepared to pay a woman who can become pregnant to have a baby for them. This is called surrogate motherhood. What are your views on surrogate motherhood? What are the arguments for allowing it? What are the arguments against it? Decide if it should be allowed.

What happens when you visit a family planning clinic?

There are over 2000 Family Planning clinics providing free contraceptive advice and supplies. Your local clinic will be in the phone directory and you just have to ring up for an appointment.

At the clinic, you'll be asked your name, address, age and the name of your doctor. It is best that your doctor knows if you're taking certain contraceptives, but the clinic will only tell him with your consent. Also, most clinics will only see girls under 16 with their parents' consent.

First, the nurse or doctor will ask questions about your health, for example, is there a history of heart disease in your family? They will then weigh you and take your blood pressure, and maybe also suggest an internal examination. This is done by feeling inside your vagina for any abnormal lumps or bumps. It's quite painless. The doctor will then tell you the different methods of contraception available and the ones they think best suited to you and your partner. Some people prefer to take their partner along too.

Different people are suited to different methods. After trying one for six months or so, you may wish to try another. You can discuss all this with the doctor at the clinic. They will show you how to use your chosen method and there are always leaflets to take home. Depending on the method you choose, you will need to go back every three, six or twelve months. For more information write to the Family Planning Association, 27-35 Mortimer Street, London W1N 7RJ (tel 01-636 7866).

PEOPLE and PREGNANCIES

Although contraceptives are efficient and freely available, the number of pregancies outside marriage has increased in recent years.

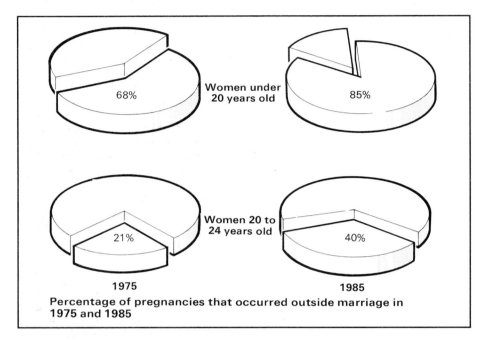

Percentage of pregnancies that occurred outside marriage in 1975 and 1985

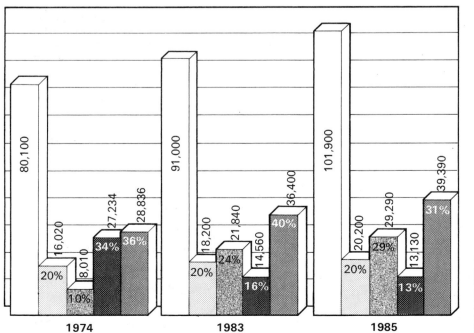

Changing trends in pregnancy.

1 Look at the pie charts on the left. Talk about the reasons for the increase in pregnancy outside of marriage. Possible points that may be included in your discussions are:
   a) There are now more sexual relationships outside marriage.
   b) People believe it can't happen to them.
   c) The effect of sex education in school.
   d) Parental control now seems to drop off at a younger age.
   e) Abortions have been easier to get.

   Do you think this trend will continue? Give reasons for your view.

2 Discuss what the figures on the left, below, show about:
   a) The rate of legal abortions 1974 and 1985.
   b) The number of women that decide to keep the child on their own (mother registers birth).
   c) The number of couples that bring up their child without getting married. (Mother and father register the birth. Let us say that this means they are raising the child together.)
   d) The number of couples that get married when, or because, the woman is pregnant.

3 Discuss why you think these changes have occurred. Your discussion may include some of the following points:
   a) Because of changing public attitudes, fewer girls need the respectability of marriage.
   b) Abortion became more readily available.
   c) There is better care and financial help for unmarried mothers (such as social security benefits).
   d) There is increasing independence for women.
   e) The influence of the church has decreased over the past generation.

All figures are for women under 20

☐ Total number of pregnancies outside marriage

☐ Mother registers birth (one-parent family)

☐ Mother and father register birth (non-married parents)

■ Mother and father marry before baby is born

▨ Number of legal abortions

Decisions about abortion

I can't possibly have you

'No woman in the world ever entered into an abortion lightheartedly. Most are genuinely upset but they *know* there was no alternative decision to be made.

I was in my forties with a grown family and a husband, also in his forties, prematurely retired from work with a life expectancy of some three years. He never knew of my pregnancy and decision to have an abortion. I could not give birth to my child and hand it to strangers for adoption. I love my children. I loved that son or daughter too. I would not risk the chance of my baby being brought up badly or cruelly or insensitively.

The night before the abortion I sat on the stairs and hugged myself and my child and said "Oh, darling, I do love you, but I can't possibly have you." I'm crying as I write this. I remember – and will never, ever forget – the day I relinquished my baby.

I've never regretted the action I took. Mourning is not necessarily regretting, you know, as anyone who has ever watched a loved-one die in pain will understand.'

We didn't know

'I was barely 15 when I became pregnant by my boyfriend. He was one year older. We were both aware of what we were doing but did not realise what could happen, as we were both very naive and uneducated about sex. I decided the best thing to do was to have an abortion. It was the biggest decision I have ever made in my life.

We were so young and I wanted to do so much with my own life. I knew I could not support myself, let alone a baby, and it would not have been fair on my parents to bring the child up for me.

I am 24 now, married to a wonderful man, who knows all about my past life and is very understanding. I will never regret the hard decision I made because I have learnt so much.

I feel a woman should be able to make the decision to have an abortion if she so wishes, because only she knows how she feels.

But if only I was told more about sex at an early age, my abortion would not have been necessary.'

A right to life

'I am shocked by the number of women who decide to have abortions. How can women be so selfish? Surely the father should have an equal right to decide the fate of his own child, and even more so the child itself has every right to life. Who are we to decide which child shall live and which shall die? There are enough families out there who would willingly bring up an unwanted child, as their own. Why do these women block out the fact they are carrying a human being?

My husband and I are both 27 and don't want children of out own. But if by chance I became pregnant, even if the foetus were known to be handicapped, we would give all the love and happiness that child would need, whatever the sacrifices.'

LEGAL ABORTIONS

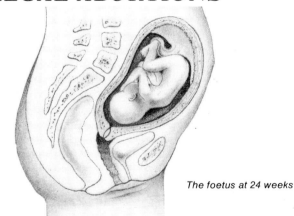

The foetus at 24 weeks

- In 1985 18% of all pregnancies ended in legal abortions. For women under 20 the figure was 39%.
- In 1988 parliament debated a bill which aimed to make abortion illegal after 18 weeks of pregnancy. The bill was not passed and the legal limit for abortions remains 28 weeks.
- Some tests to discover severe handicaps and abnormalities cannot be effectively carried out before 18 weeks.
- One amendment to the 1988 bill (which there was not time to debate) suggested a limit of 24 weeks.
- At 24 weeks the foetus (unborn baby) measures about 30 centimetres.
- Babies have sometimes survived when born after 24 weeks of pregnancy.

IN GROUPS

1 What do you think is shown by the number of abortions carried out in 1985? Do you think fewer women would have abortions if they knew more about safe methods of contraception?

2 The chances of permanent damage, infertility, and even death are increased in illegal abortions by unqualified people. These are called 'backstreet' abortions. With this in mind, decide in which of the following situations abortion should be legal:

a) On demand by the mother.
b) If an extra child would cause hardship.
c) If the parents could not or would not look after the child properly.
d) If the child would be born with severe physical and/or mental handicap.
e) If continued pregnancy would endanger the life of the mother.
f) If the pregnancy resulted from rape.
g) If the child were infected by AIDS in the womb.
h) Any other reason(s).
i) Under no circumstances.

Share your decisions, giving reasons, with the other groups.

FOR YOUR FOLDER

Write a brief summary of your views on abortion.
Why do you think people choose abortion rather than having the baby and putting it up for adoption?

Caring
for your unborn child

▶ *Caring for a baby does not start only when it is born. If a child is to have the best chance of growing up healthy, care should begin at the time of conception. This is not down only to the mother-to-be. The support and understanding of her partner is an important part of this care.*

How the baby develops

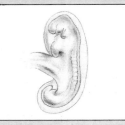

Weeks 4-5
Formation of the neural tube that will become the brain and spinal cord. The heart and blood vessels forming. Cells in position to form other vital organs.

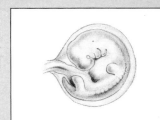

Weeks 6-7
Brain developing and heart begins to beat. Ears and eyes starting to develop along with first bones and muscles. Limb buds for arms and legs appearing. Size at 7 weeks about 8 mm.

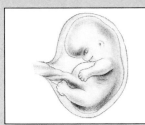

Weeks 8-9
Major internal organs developing along with face, eyes and mouth. Hands and feet developing as ridges at the end of arms and legs. Size at 9 weeks about 17 mm.

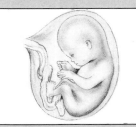

Weeks 10-14
At about 12 weeks the foetus is fully formed. Sex organs are well developed. From now on organs mature, the baby gains weight, nails grow and finger prints form. Size about 56 mm.

The placenta allows passage of:

Food and oxygen from mother's blood stream.

Waste and carbon dioxide to mother's blood stream.

Alcohol, nicotine and other drugs?

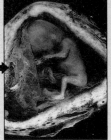

Warning from a packet of cigarettes

Warning: SMOKING WHEN PREGNANT CAN INJURE YOUR BABY AND CAUSE PREMATURE BIRTH
Health Departments' Chief Medical Officers

Some questions

Should I smoke during pregnancy?

Your baby gets less oxygen than it should if you smoke. Smoking cuts down the supply of oxygen for a long time after the cigarette has been finished. There is a higher risk of complications at birth. There is a higher risk that the baby will be premature. There is a higher risk that the baby will be underweight. The nicotine will make the baby's heart beat too fast. Secondary smoking (breathing smoke from other people's cigarettes) will also affect your baby in a similar way.

Is drinking alcohol also dangerous?

Foetal Alcohol Syndrome affects one in three babies born to mothers with an alcohol problem. The baby may be very small. It may have reduced intelligence. It may be born with facial deformities. Foetal Alcohol Syndrome will not affect babies whose mothers only drink a little but even light to moderate drinking is now thought to be bad for the baby.

Are pills and medicine I decide to take myself of any harm?

A wide number of drugs, including those that can be bought without a prescription, can have a harmful effect on the baby, especially early in pregnancy.

It is advised that all drugs, unless prescribed by a doctor, should be avoided. It is probably safe to take the occasional paracetamol or aspirin for a headache or other pain, but not in early pregnancy.

What sort of foods should I eat when I'm pregnant?

Your diet is important to the development of the baby. You need to eat a variety of foods. You should cut back on sugary or fatty foods and eat plenty of fruit and vegetables (for vitamins); meat, fish and eggs (for protein) and milk or cheese (for calcium). Folic acid (found in liver and cabbage) is also important.

Planning ahead

It is the early months of pregnancy that are especially important. In the twelve weeks after conception, all the baby's organs are formed, including the brain, the nervous system and the heart. Yet during this vital early time you may not even know you are pregnant.

So, since no couple can know exactly when they will conceive, it makes sense to 'prepare' for pregnancy. Then you can be certain that from the moment of conception onwards you will be giving your baby the best possible chance of being healthy. And you will be less likely to be worried or anxious during pregnancy.

More questions

How much weight should I put on during pregnancy?

The quality of what you eat during pregnancy is now considered more important than the quantity, although no pregnant woman should skimp on meals. Weight gain varies from woman to woman but a woman of average build will probably gain about 24lbs. The increase is only partly fat; the rest is accounted for by the baby, the fluid surrounding it, the placenta, larger breasts and womb and increased blood circulation. If you are underweight when you become pregnant, you are at higher risk of having a low birthweight baby, more prone to infections. Increasing your intake of the right foods during pregnancy will lower the risks by half. There can also be complications if you are overweight when you become pregnant, such as a higher chance of needing a Caesarean birth. You should not diet but you should definitely not overeat.

Is it safe to dye my hair? I've heard it can cause birth defects.

The coal tar chemicals in permanent and semi-permanent dyes and rinses can penetrate the scalp and enter the bloodstream. These chemicals have been linked to chromosomal damage and cell change, so the possible dangers must be considered. But, as yet there is no solid proof that hair dye can be linked to birth defects.

Rinses don't seem to be as potentially harmful as permanent and semi-permanent dyes, may be, because the coal tar chemicals in rinses coat the hair shafts rather than penetrating the scalp. Techniques which only involve the shafts, such as hair tipping and streaking, are safer than permanent and semi-permanent one-colour processes. Henna, a non-chemical, natural, reddish-brown dye, would be the safest.

I suggest you avoid all hair colouring in the first three months, when the brain and nervous system of the foetus are developing. After that, risk is reduced, but for safety, you might consider postponing dyeing your hair until after the birth of your baby.

Is exercise a good idea during pregnancy?

During a problem-free pregnancy, moderate exercise is definitely desirable. It can ease lower back pain and leg cramps, improve circulation and strengthen the pelvic floor muscles ready for childbirth. Also, if you keep in trim during pregnancy, it is easier to get back into shape after it. But don't overdo it. When you exercise during pregnancy, you elevate an already high heart rate. You may also pull ligaments more easily, as they soften during pregnancy.

I advise women with a history of miscarriage to exercise very little during the first three months, when risk of miscarriage is highest. Later, when the foetus is firmly implanted in the womb, exercise can ease the strain of expectancy. Exercises using smooth movements – such as walking, swimming, on-the-spot cycling – are best.

A woman with high risk pregnancy complications should not exercise at all.

HUMAN RIGHTS

Article 2 of the UN Declaration of Human Rights (1948)

'Everyone is entitled to all the rights and freedoms set forth in this Declaration, without distinction of any kind, such as race, colour . . .'

South Africa follows a system called apartheid. This involves segregating different groups of the population – keeping white and black people strictly apart socially, economically and culturally. Although black people total 74% of the population only 13% of the land is set aside for them to occupy. Those who work and live away from their area are ruled by severe laws which restrict their freedom of movement. Because they have to live outside of areas where whites live, they often have long trips to get to their work. There are many laws that prevent mixing of whites and blacks. These for examples forbid whites and blacks using the same park benches, restaurants, beaches and buses in many areas. Almost all schools and most hospitals are segregated. Hospitals and schools for blacks are usually poorly funded and badly equipped.

This clearly does not follow the ideals of Article 2 of the UN Declaration of Human Rights (1948). Although some of the laws have been changed over the past few years, mainly through the black struggle, there is still a long way to go. What good is being able to play in the same cricket team if you and your family usually don't have access to decent sports facilities? When will blacks get promotion to senior jobs in industry instead of doing the most menial jobs in the factories and mines?

The continuing opposition of the blacks to apartheid is cruelly and harshly met by the police and army. Even peaceful demonstrations often result in the death of many of the demonstrators. Many of the black leaders have been imprisoned. The most famous of these is Nelson Mandela, who has been in confinement since 1962, in spite of world opinion calling for his release. Winnie Mandela, his wife, is a leader of the struggle in her own right. She has been continually harassed by the government, and all her movements have been controlled and restricted.

Here are some of the arguments given in support of apartheid.

- The development of South Africa into the richest country in Africa has been due to the white people, so they should be allowed to reap the benefits of their work.
- The cultures of the black and the white people are different and it has been proved that they can't live peacefully together.
- Most black people in South Africa have a higher standard of living than people in other African countries.
- In many other African countries independence and black majority rule have led to regional feuds. The result has been unrest and inequality.

IN GROUPS

1 Discuss the arguments given in support of apartheid. Should people with different cultures (ways of living) live separately? Have the whites the sole right to benefit from their efforts in developing the country? How good is the argument that the black people in South Africa have a higher standard of living than blacks in other countries of Africa? Is there any justification for the majority to be ruled by a minority? Produce a group list of arguments to put *against* each of those given in support of apartheid.

2 Do you think a white South African would agree with the message given by the drawing? How do you think they see themselves?

3 Put yourselves in the place of a black South African. Why would you think that apartheid is unjust?

4 There is no official apartheid in Britain. Does this mean that the blacks and Asians always get fair treatment: **a)** under the law; **b)** from other people?

Share your views in a class discussion.

Article 19 of the UN Declaration of Human Rights (1948)

'Everyone has the right to freedom of opinion and expression; this right includes freedom to hold opinions without interference...'

In the Soviet Union the law forbids anti-Soviet opinions and membership of anti-Soviet organisations. What this means, in effect, is that it is illegal to criticise or to demonstrate against the government's policies.

People run the risk of arrest for such actions as: giving certain reasons for wanting to emigrate; writing letters of complaint to the authorities; speaking out against the Soviet Union or its policies. People are also restricted in their practice of religion: they may be arrested for printing bibles. Very rarely does anyone charged with political or religious offences go free after a trial.

Punishments can vary and are often severe. They include confinement in prison camps, often in cold and far away areas; treatment in a mental hospital; internal exile in cut-off places; normal prison sentences. The actual sentence often comes after much police harassment.

The story of one man can be used to illustrate the denial of human rights in the Soviet Union. Alexander Solzhenitsyn was sentenced to eight years in a 'corrective' camp at the end of World War II for criticising the Russian leader, Stalin, in letters to a friend. At the end of his ordeal, he started to write books about his experiences, following which he underwent many years of harassment. He even feared for his life.

His books were published in the West, and in 1970 he was awarded the Nobel Prize, the highest honour a writer can get. When his new book on conditions in Soviet labour camps was published in 1973, he was arrested, charged with treason, stripped of his citizenship and exiled to the West.

Recently under the leadership of Mikhail Gorbachev more freedom of expression has been permitted. However there is still a long way to go.

Here are some of the arguments given in support of Soviet ideas on human rights.

- The Soviet state looks after its people all through their lives.
- Many prices are fixed, unemployment is unknown and the people are safe from outside attack. Surely this is more important than the freedom of an individual to criticise the system? What good is freedom of any kind if you are unemployed and living in poverty?
- Freedom of expression is allowed providing it is in the interests of the Soviet people and system.
- The state is simply protecting the rights of all citizens by preventing anyone from undermining the system on which they depend.

IN GROUPS

1 Discuss the arguments given in support of Soviet laws that prevent people criticising the government and its system. Would you prefer to be assured of a job at the cost of being able to speak your mind? Or do you feel both things are equally important? Which is the most important, the individual or the state? What do you think of the methods which we hear the Soviet Union uses to silence people who disagree with the state?

2 In Britain, groups such as the various Communist Parties and the National Front are allowed to express their opinions. Before reading this case study, did you think that the Communist and other left-wing political parties in Britain should be given full freedom to criticise the government? If so, do you still think so after reading the piece? What about right-wing groups like the National Front?

3 Why do you think that Alexander Solzhenitsyn was exiled to the West rather than sent back to a labour camp or given another punishment?

FOR YOUR FOLDER

In London at Hyde Park there is an area called Speaker's Corner. Here anyone can make a speech in public about anything they want to, be it nuclear missiles or the price of a pint of beer. Write a short statement for your folder on whether you would be likely to find a Speaker's Corner in South Africa and the Soviet Union.

Global inequality

Most people in Britain would not consider themselves rich. Compared to many other countries, however, we are rich: rich in how much we produce, in education, in industry, in housing, in food, in water, in health – in fact, in almost everything.

The wealth of a country can be measured by its Gross National Product (GNP), which is the value of all goods and services produced in the country. The greater the GNP, the better the living standards of the people in that country should be.

Below are some examples of the GNP per person in 1984 for Britain and some of the other countries of the world.

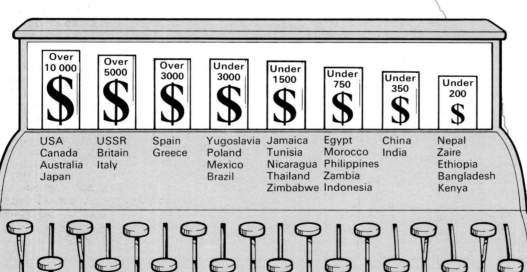

Over 10 000 $	Over 5000 $	Over 3000 $	Under 3000 $	Under 1500 $	Under 750 $	Under 350 $	Under 200 $
USA Canada Australia Japan	USSR Britain Italy	Spain Greece	Yugoslavia Poland Mexico Brazil	Jamaica Tunisia Nicaragua Thailand Zimbabwe	Egypt Morocco Philippines Zambia Indonesia	China India	Nepal Zaire Ethiopia Bangladesh Kenya

Money available for developing industry, education, defence, agriculture, health care, housing, transport, modernisation, water and sanitation, communications, among other things.

Examples of GNP per person per year in 1984 (in USA$)

'In order to buy the things they need like clothes and education farmers in developing countries are forced to grow cash crops so they can't grow enough food.'

'They seem to have enough money to raise armies. They should use that for development.'

'Depending on how much it can afford, each country should pay a certain amount each year to help poorer countries.'

'Whereas I have sympathy with drought victims, homeless refugees and, to a lesser degree, AIDS victims, I feel I cannot tolerate the decline in the National Health Service any longer. The old saying "charity begins at home" must surely have some relevance to this situation.'

'Most people in Britain are willing to contribute something to developing countries. Just look at Live Aid and Comic Relief.'

'Why can't they look after themselves? We do in Britain!'

'To really help the poorer countries we will need to cut our own standard of living.'

'The British Empire contributed to many problems in developing countries. Britain has a responsibility to try and help solve them.'

'I don't know anything about their problems. Why should I care?'

'Many developing countries are poor because the richer countries who need their raw materials, won't pay a fair price for them.'

'They're already taking jobs from our country by providing cheap labour in their new factories. Why should we help?'

Should we help?

IN GROUPS

1 Consider the information given on the cash register opposite and the facts about life in a country with a low GNP. Then study and discuss each of the above comments. Decide which you: **1)** strongly agree with; **2)** agree with in part; **3)** disagree in part; **4)** strongly disagree with. Based on your discussion, produce a statement about whether you think that Britain should or should not help the poorer countries of the world.

2 Do you think Band Aid and Comic Relief helped to make people more aware of the needs of poorer countries? Why do you think the stars participated in these events?

FOR YOUR FOLDER

Design a poster to make people think about global inequality and what they can do about it. You can use words or pictures, or both.

Caring about conservation

More and more demands are being made on the land. Is it being used in the interest of all, or is it being wasted and even destroyed? Look at and think about these examples:

Poor soils are over-used

In many areas, poor people are pushed onto the poorest lands. In order to grow enough to eat, they are forced to overwork the soil. They also raise the same crops every year. In this way, hillsides are being worn away, and once grassy plains are turning to dust.

Land is wasted

In some parts of the world large areas of land are not farmed. These are in the hands of companies and rich people who like to own land, even though they may not need to use it all at any one time.

The growth of towns

The world's towns and cities grow by eating up the countryside. Huge areas of good farming land are lost each year to houses, factories, roads and airports.

Single crop cultivation

Commercial farmers also grow the same crop year after year, but they do so to meet market demands. They keep their yields high by using large amounts of fertiliser. Experts warn that this is likely to destroy important nutrients in the soil.

Destruction of trees

Trees protect the land. Their roots hold the soil and their leaves shield it from the hot sun or heavy rain. Yet acres of forest have been destroyed in recent years, mainly by people who make money from the wood, or use the cleared land for raising cattle.

The effects of pollution

In industrialised countries, land has been lost and rivers ruined through the careless dumping of harmful wastes. Forests in Europe and North America have been damaged by acid rain, which comes from air and water pollution.

1 Study the pictures on the left and their captions. Which example of bad practice concerns you most? Act out a scene in which a person who cares about conservation tries to persuade someone with the attitude: 'Why should I care?' that they *should* be concerned. What world conservation issues affect us all? Why is it important to support conservation policies?

2 In Britain, there are thousands of acres of wasteland in and around our towns and cities. These lie unused, even though they could be used for homes and public buildings. What wasteland is there in and around your area? Are there any plans to use such land to make your area a better place to live? Suggest ways in which the wasteland could be redeveloped. Then, join another pair and discuss your suggestions.

Priorities

In countries where people expect a high standard of living, there are many different views on how land should be used. Do we in Britain always use our living space in the best possible way?

certain way of using land? On your own, look at the eight development proposals. Write down any that you have strong enough feelings about to make you join a protest. Then, in your group, compare your lists and discuss your reasons.

Said Somebody

Said Somebody:
The trees, of course,
will have to be chopped down
and we'll build the road
across some farm land

Said Somebody else:
It would be easier to use the cricket field
We could build fifty houses there –
back to back, of course.
It's only used in summer anyway.

Said Somebody:
There might be objections,
and we've got our seats to consider

Well, said Somebody else:
How about that bit of scruffy Green Belt
or the National Trust Park
– or with a wink in the right direction
something could be arranged.
And after all, we do need houses
and laundrettes and pubs and streetlights . . .

Trouble is, said Somebody,
They've got their priorities all wrong
– think trees and fields and birds
are more important than rooves
over people's heads

If we're not careful, said Somebody,
we'll have the cranks out
with their placards again.
By the way,
Does anybody know what 'Ecology' means?

Tina Morris

1 Tearing down a pair of medieval cottages, which are of historic and architectural value, to make way for a new road.

2 Siting a new airport on local farmland.

3 Starting to mine coal on the site of a local area noted for its natural beauty.

4 Making a dump for low-level nuclear waste in disused mineshafts in your locality.

5 A local farmer planning to destroy a marshland, where a very rare species of plant is found, to farm it.

6 Building a new hospital on land which is part of the 'green belt', or area of open land meant to remain natural.

7 Building a military camp on local moorland and using the whole area as a training centre, closing it to the public.

8 Creating a new reservoir by flooding an area which is a breeding ground for a rare species of bird.

3 A local industrialist has left £5 million in her will, to be spent on a project 'for the conservation of the local environment.' You are the trustees responsible for deciding and overseeing the project. Draft a plan, explaining how you would spend the money. Appoint a spokesperson to present your idea to the rest of the class. When all the groups have presented their ideas, hold a class discussion and reach a decision on which plan to support.

1 Discuss Tina Morris's poem. What points about development and conservation is she trying to make? What do you think her priorities are?

2 What are your views about people who make protests on conservation issues? Do you regard them as cranks? Would you ever be willing to protest against a plan for a

FOR YOUR FOLDER

Write a statement saying which conservation issues you are most concerned about and why. Or write a letter to your local newspaper stating your views on one issue that you feel strongly about.

A PERSONAL RECORD

The aim of this unit is to give you the opportunity to write a statement which you can keep as a personal record of your achievements, both inside and outside school.

There are three stages you will need to follow in preparing your statement. The first is to carry out a review of your achievements. The second is to see your tutor with a first draft of your statement and discuss it together. The third is to write the final version of the statement.

STAGE 1
A REVIEW OF YOUR ACHIEVEMENTS

Make notes about what you have achieved both in and out of school during your five years of secondary school. List your achievements under headings such as: GCSE courses; TVEI courses; school activities (sport, music, drama, clubs and societies); work experience, residential experiences, outings and visits; out of school interests (part-time jobs, clubs, evening and weekend activities).

Refer to the statements you wrote at the end of each of the previous four years, the CV you prepared earlier this year, and details of your own particular strengths which you identified during self-assessment exercises. Include everything which you consider to be an achievement. The aim is to show a complete record.

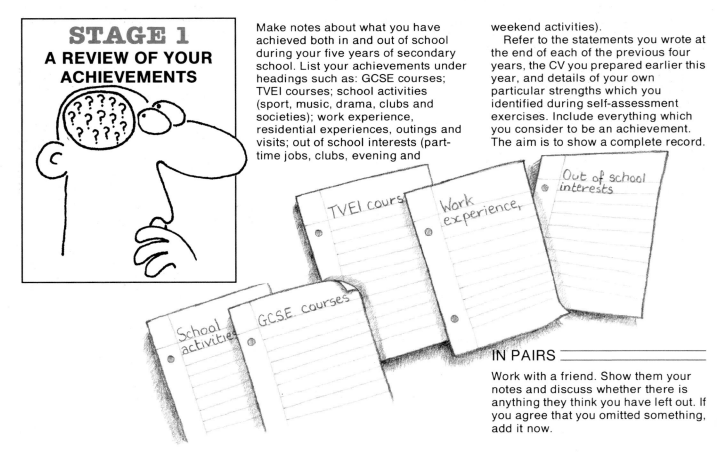

IN PAIRS

Work with a friend. Show them your notes and discuss whether there is anything they think you have left out. If you agree that you omitted something, add it now.

Prepare a draft of your statement and show it to your tutor. Discuss exactly what you are planning to put in, and add anything which your tutor suggests you should add.

STAGE 3
WRITING THE STATEMENT

Write out you final statement and give it to your tutor. They will sign it to certify that it is an accurate record of your achievements during your school career. This can be neatly handwritten in ink, typed or printed out on a word processor.

BRYAN

This is the final statement written by a student in his last year at secondary school after discussions with his teacher.

During the last two years at Ridgeway Castle I think I have learned a lot of things and I think I have grown up since the fourth year. The fourth year wasn't too good for me and the fifth year has been better. The teachers also get better when you get older and treat you better.

I like sport and enjoy badminton and tennis a lot.

I sometimes find difficulties in lessons but I don't let it bother me. I think the school is good at organising trips, res. ed. and work experience.

I went to Kettlewell in Yorkshire and I did ponytrekking, cycling, walking, football, rounders, swimming, map reading, visits and caving; we also went to Morecambe for the day.

I didn't enjoy my work experience much, but I'm glad I did it because I found I definitely didn't want to do nursery work. But I think work experience is a good idea. I like doing TVEI because of the ten week modules, so if you pick one and you don't like it you only have to take it for ten weeks and not two years like other subjects.

On Thursday nights I come to school to do badminton. I like this a lot. My other hobbies are acting, reading, watching television, going out, listening to music.

When I leave school I hope to get on a catering YTS and then get a job after that. I know it is going to be hard, but I am prepared to try. I want to leave school, but at the same time I will be sad to leave my mates, but I shall see them out of school.

Acknowledgements

The following publishers, authors and agents are thanked for the permission to reproduce extracts and copyright material:
Jenny Tucker, published by Virgin Books a division of W. H. Allen & Co Plc, (p 2); *City Close Up Blackburn* by Jeremy Seabrook, Penguin Books, (p 2); How do you know if it's really love? by Claire Rayner, *Woman's Own*, 3 November 1984, (p 3); Bristol Broadsides from *Let's Hurry Up and Get This Relationship Over . . . So I Can Get on With Decorating the Hallway*, (1987), (p 3); *True to Life* edited by Susan Hemmings and *Girls are Powerful,* Sheba, (p 5); Sex Before Marriage, (p 8); Do You Believe in God? (pp 16 and 17) and extracts from articles on Politics, (p 38), Nuclear Defence, (p 40), Models, (p 55), all from *Just Seventeen;* Aids poster, Health Education Authority, (p 9); Buddy Can You Spare the Time? by Adam Marrs Jones issue May 1987, and an article on pregnancy (pp 68 and 69) both from *Cosmopolitan; Doing Social Science Reserach – A Guide to Coursework* by Peter Langley (p 11), and *Politics A New Approach* by David Roberts (p 45), both from Causeway Books; Getting Down to Work adapted from *Teaching Study Skills* by Douglas H. Hamblin (pp 12 and 46), Learning from Examinations in *Learn How to Study* by D. Rowntree (pp 13 and 47), from Blackwell Ltd; What is your moral value? adapted from *The Book of Tests* by Dr. Michael Nathenson (Fontana), (p 15); *Cheque-In Magazine,* Midland Bank, (pp 18 and 19, 26 and 27, 33 and 34); Leaving Home adapted from *Leaving Home* by Mark Clark and Alan Dearling (p 20), Needs and Expectations from a leaflet *'Young Homelessness'* (p 21) both from Shelter; Young and Homeless from *Homes and Homelessness* in Bother No 147, Oxfam, (pp 22 and 23); captions from the information leaflet *Poverty and Power,* Oxfam, (p 74); Consumer Rights article from *Woman,* 10 January 1987, (p 23); Only Themselves to Blame – from an article 2 February 1986, Mail Newspapers Plc; Rejection Case Studies and The Rejection Trap (p 34), What Happens When You Visit a Family Planning Clinic? (p 65), all extracts from *Mizz* issues 35 and 46; *Letters to Judy Blume* (p 36), *Health and Safety at Work* by Eva Oswald (p 60) both Pan Books Ltd; Your Political Views, extracts from issue 7 January 1987, (p 39), Whose Got You on File? issue 9 November 1987, *The Guardian; The Arms Race* by John Turner from Cambridge University Press, (p 41); *Social Issues: The World* by J. M. Coults by Heinemann Educational, (p 43); Data Protection leaflet, adapted from Data Protection Registrar, (pp 48 and 49); Page Three Girls issue 26 August-1 September 1987, *Best,* (p 55); All Our Own Work, Manpower Services Commission, (pp 56 and 57); TUC Guidelines on Protecting Young People at Work, (p. 60); 'Moterbike gear' poster, Royal Society for the Prevention of Accidents, (p 62), Learning for Change in World Society, *The Ecologist,* (p 75); Student Reviewing and Recording from the "OCEA Teacher Guide", University of Oxford, (p 77).

Illustrators

Andrew Aloof pp 35, 41; Elaine Andersen pp 67, 68; Michael Armson p 22; Lorraine Calaora p. 58; Jerry Collins all torn edge shadows and pp 4, 5, 6, 8, 9, 21, 25, 26, 42, 43, 46, 52, 54, 60, 66, 72; Lizzie Kelsall p 19; Patrick McAllister pp 50, 51; Gillian Martin pp 20, 24, 44, 69; Peter Schrank pp 32, 43, 70, 71; Nick Sharratt p 3; Martin Shovel pp 48, 49, 76; Bill Stott pp 47, 61, 63; Hany Tamba pp 10, 30.

Photographs

All photographs N. Fyson except p 2 Dave Scammell; p 16 left Simone Berg, centre and right *Just 17;* p 17 left Steve Rapport, right Tim Bauer; p 19 Midland Bank *Cheque In;* p 25 Anne Barrowclough; p 33 Midland Bank *Cheque In;* p 52 BBC Hulton; p 55 Rex Feature; p 59 top and bottom Chris Davies/Network, centre Laurie Sparham/Network; p 63 Sally and Richard Greenhill; p 68 Science Photo Library; p 74 top left Mike Goldwater/Network, top centre The National Trust, top right and bottom left Tony and Marion Morrison, bottom centre Barry Lewis/Network, bottom right Sally and Richard Greenhill.

Cover photograph courtesy of Hollyfield Secondary School, Surbiton.

The authors and publishers are grateful to the staff and pupils at Rooks Heath School, South Harrow for their help with the photographs.

Every effort has been made to contact the holders of copyright material but if any have been inadvertently overlooked the publishers will be pleased to make the necessary arrangements at the first opportunity.